ON
GOVERNMENT
SPENDING

by

Robert L. Heilbroner

&

Peter L. Bernstein

VINTAGE BOOKS

A *Division of Random House*

NEW YORK

FIRST VINTAGE EDITION, MAY, 1963

VINTAGE BOOKS
*are published by Alfred A. Knopf, Inc.
and Random House, Inc.*

Library of Congress Catalog Card Number: 63-16856

MANUFACTURED IN THE UNITED STATES OF AMERICA

HERBERT J. GOODMAN AND JOHN K. WEISS

In Memoriam

❧ Contents

A Primer on Government Spending

❧ I

Preface

This book springs from the belief that many people are worried about government spending—worried about what it may do to our currency, worried about what it may do to our economy, and above all, worried because they know they do not understand the very thing they are worried about.

It is understandable that government spending should conjure up these worries, for it deals in a lexicon of worrisome terms—debts and deficits—and talks in a language of profligacy—tens and hundreds of billions of dollars. Worse yet, it asks us to consider these unsettling words and these inconceivable sums in relation to a range of economic problems that also worry us because we grasp them only uncertainly: inflation, unemployment, automation, economic growth.

Much of this worry is unnecessary. It stems not from the genuine problems of government spending, but from a lack of understanding that distorts and grotesquely magnifies those problems. Hence the purpose of this primer is to spell out the meaning of the words that frighten us—government spending, deficit financing, the national debt, growth, inflation—in clear, vivid, and, above all, simple terms. For the basic ideas of government spending are relatively easy to grasp. The challenge they present to the reader is not to perform feats of mental gymnastics, but to entertain a new point of view; not to learn the skills and techniques of an economist, but only to share his unaccustomed vantage point.

It is hardly out of a desire to popularize economic thinking that we have written this introduction to government spending. It is rather from a profound belief that the deliberate, intelligent, and thoughtful employment of the economic power of government is of paramount importance for the nation. If the argument of this book is correct, the well-being of millions of Americans will be directly affected by the use they make of the government as a force for economic advancement. And the use they make of the government will in turn be directly affected by the understanding they possess about the government as an economic force.

Where to exert the power of government and how to control it are surely among the most crucially important questions that the American people must answer over the coming years. They are questions involving political issues of great moment—issues about which reasonable men can reasonably disagree. Yet even the most reasonable men will never settle these issues intelligently if they say unreasonable things about the purely *economic* matters at stake.

But what things are unreasonable?

"At the heart of our national finances," declared Representative Clarence Cannon (Dem., Mo.), Chairman of the House Appropriations Committee, on January 17, 1963, the day President Kennedy startled the nation by proposing a deliberate budget deficit of $10,000,-000,000, "is a simple, inescapable fact, easily grasped by anyone. It is that our Government—any government—like individuals and families—cannot spend and continue to spend more than they take in without inviting disaster. With governments, continued deficit spending inevitably leads to debasement of the currency. A dollar is only as valuable and reliable as it is to us."

These do not, surely, seem to be the sentiments of unreason. Indeed, the Congressman's concern was widely echoed throughout the country. "Item by item," wrote Arthur Krock, senior Washington correspondent for the *New York Times*, "the budget reflects the incessantly disproved economic theory that government can bestow all these material benefits without a grim reckoning at any time in the future." All over the country newspaper editors nervously asked their readers, "Can we afford this deficit?" and concluded that we could not. Perhaps most impressive of all was the response reported by Congresswoman Martha Griffiths of Detroit to a questionnaire she sent to her constituents, asking what they would do with a possible tax reduction of $100. Of the thousand who replied to her letter, six hundred said *they did not want a tax cut if it meant unbalancing the budget.*

"Ask not what your country can do for you, but what you can do for your country," President Kennedy had exhorted the public in his Inaugural Address. Now the public had found an answer. It could prevent the government from going bankrupt.

These are undeniably persuasive voices. Who can look on a budget such as that proposed by President Kennedy, with its expenditures totaling $120,000,000,-000, its gigantic deficit, its apparent unconcern about adding to a national debt already $304,000,000,000 high, and not feel concerned? Who cannot picture to himself the end result of such reckless spending and heedless borrowing for any family? Who does not grasp the elementary logic of Dickens' Mr. Micawber: "Annual income twenty pounds, annual expenditure nineteen pounds, nineteen shillings and sixpence: result, happiness. Annual income twenty pounds, annual expenditure twenty pounds, no shillings and sixpence: result, misery."

And yet there is an element of perplexity here. Surely there are few, no matter how vehement their objections to deficit spending, who would accuse the President and his advisers of *seeking* the financial ruination of the United States. There are, we are aware, other voices, perhaps less resonant against the public sounding board, who tell us differently about the problem of government spending—the members of the President's Council of Economic Advisers, or Walter Lippmann in his political columns, or a number of distinguished foreign economic observers. These people assure us that a deficit is not dangerous, that our national debt is not a burden, that government spending will not lead to disastrous consequences. On the contrary, they tell us that if we are to move an object as vast, as planetary as our economy, only the judicious use of government spending will give the Archimedean leverage we need.

It is surely very hard for the interested bystander to know what to think. On the one hand there are the expressions of alarm and distrust that appeal directly to his own experience—the manifest impossibility of running his own financial affairs in the way that the government is evidently trying to run its own. On the other hand, men of responsibility tell him that there is nothing to be alarmed about, and that he should not confuse his own financial situation with that of the government. Indeed, they tell him that when he pictures the problem in the terms most familiar to him, it only shows that he doesn't know what the issue is really all about.

With that last the bystander—who is most of us— is quick to agree. But how to come to grips with this seemingly complicated question? How to find a way of looking at the national economy through eyes other than those of a financially prudent householder? One thing is very clear. We will never see the problem from our normal economic vantage point, at sea level. If we are to begin to understand the national issue of government spending we must mount to a height which will give us a national perspective, and from this elevated perch look out over a grandiose sight which rolls into view.

❧ II

Wealth and Waste

What do we see from this extraordinary perspective? The spectacle is much like that available to a traveler who crosses the United States by airplane. Looking down from an economic bird's-eye view, we see at first a vast panorama, natural and man-made: houses, stores, factories, mines, schools; rail lines, power lines, phone lines; dams, docks, machinery of a thousand kinds; cars, TV antennas, wash hanging out to dry; horses, cows, chickens; wheat growing in fields, the forest land —a landscape that interests us, however, not in its aesthetic aspects, but solely insofar as it evidences another quality. All of this is our national wealth. It is what is left of everything we have wrested from the earth, assembled and accumulated during our entire

national economic history. It is the arsenal of our economic strength.

The arsenal is estimated to be worth $2,000,000,000,-
000. But gazing down on this accumulation of things,
we cannot help noticing something else. It is that in
our inventory of the nation's assets we have noticed no
money, stocks, bonds, mortgages, deeds, or certificates
of ownership of any kind.

This failure to include our stocks and bonds and
money is strange. When we are at economic sea level
there is no doubt that it is by just such certificates that
we count our individual wealth. Yet from our elevated
vantage, we can see that these certificates are nonetheless different from wealth. They are *claims* against
wealth, establishing the legal right of person X to
property Y, dividing up otherwise indivisible assets,
such as steel plants, into convenient "shares." Even our
money—coin and currency and bank deposits—cannot
be counted as part of our national wealth, for it too only
establishes the right of money-holders to participate in
the division of our national output. If we had only
money we would be as poor as Midas.

We shall return later to the relationship between our
national wealth and its paper representation, but one
conclusion must already be clear. Our real wealth lies in
the landscape of assets spread out before our gaze—to
which must be added the still more valuable inventory
of human beings within that landscape, together with
all their skills, knowledge, habits, drives. Increasing or
decreasing the claims to that wealth, printing or de-
stroying money, mortgages, bonds, or stocks will not in
itself add or subtract one iota from the aggregate of
real wealth. Additional certificates of various kinds can

rearrange the pattern of claims, weakening the hold of person X on property Y, or forcing the previous sharers of the steel mill to admit others to a claim on the property. But wealth itself can be neither created nor abolished by paper manipulation alone.

But the panorama of wealth is not the only vista to reveal itself to our economic overview. Equally important is a second extraordinary sight that is also invisible at sea level. This is a vast process that we see taking place between the assets and their human possessors. The assets by themselves are silent and sterile, the human beings by themselves weak and ineffective, but the combination of the two resembles a kind of chemical reaction in which an inert substance and a weak reagent combine to deliver an explosive result. For as we watch the economic landscape we can see a continuous interaction between men and their land and capital—an interaction that brings forth a tremendous outpouring of *new* wealth, which we call our output, or our production.

And finally, to complete the drama, we must follow the new wealth that is continually being created. Most of it seems to disappear. Emerging in one moment from the interplay of the land, our labor, and our capital assets, it is consumed in the next moment, partly to replenish and refresh the human beings who divide up this production among themselves as their income, partly to restore and reconstitute those parts of our national wealth that have themselves become used up by virtue of their participation in the production cycle. And yet normally there is something left over. If we watch the interaction of men and wealth for a full period—say a year—we see that not all the new wealth is consumed. A part is normally added to the vast stock of wealth itself, so that in the next period of productive interaction men will cooperate with even greater stores of wealth and thus supply themselves even more richly.

A first overview of the productive process cannot fail to impress an observer. But what strikes us as we survey the current scene is not alone the grandiose process by which men and wealth cooperate to produce new wealth, but the puzzling fact that not all men and not all wealth are engaged in this cycle of renewal and increase. In fact as we peer down upon the United States we can see that substantial quantities of our wealth—blast furnaces, looms, machine tools, paper-making machinery, office space—are standing idle or being used at far less than capacity. The mere presence of wealth, in other words, is no guarantee that its productive powers will in fact be used.

Thus it is not only wealth but waste that springs to view in a survey of the national economy. Over the past five years at least $150 billions of goods and services could have been produced—but were not. This is waste on a monumental scale. But of all the forms of waste, by far the cruelest and the most costly is the waste of human resources. A machine left idle may deteriorate and by its sheer inactivity penalize the productivity of society. But a man left idle is deprived of his claim on society's output, and unless he is supported by his community he will starve. Unemployment, particularly for the least educated, least skilled, least propertied—who are the most likely to be unemployed—is the most angering, humiliating, and frightening experience that "normal" life in our society has to offer.

Nevertheless, unemployment was the reality of daily experience for nearly five million people in the United States in early 1963. This is a large enough number so that if it affected the other end of the income scale— if by some quirk of economic mischief it was the rich who were unemployed and not the poor—virtually every person in the nation earning $15,000 or more would be without a job.

And the *trend* of unemployment is even more disquieting than the number. In 1952 our economy operated at very nearly full employment. That is, anyone who wanted work for which he was qualified was more or less certain to find such work. Only two million of our labor force—one out of every thirty-three working people—were unemployed, and this probably represented the hard core of "unemployables" and the useful *voluntary* unemployment associated with job shifting.

Two years later, however, the number had grown by over a million. Almost three million men and women were without work for substantial periods of time, and during the brief 1954 recession this number rose to three and a half million. By 1958 another recession had brought unemployment up to 4.7 million— an alarming figure. But the pool of idle men receded again as business improved—this time, however, to a new level, a million higher than after the previous recession.

In early 1963 the upward creep continued. The number of unemployed was now high—over four million and threatening to top five million—and the increase was beginning to cluster disturbingly in the younger age brackets. For a semiskilled factory worker, the chances of unemployment were about one in thirteen, but for a young person just out of school and looking for a job, they were one in seven—and if the youth was a Negro, one in *four*.

And still the threat mounts. For all during the 1960s and the 1970s the number of young job seekers is going to grow, as the baby boom of the 1940s reaches employable age. If we are going to find jobs for these relatively untrained—and potentially disruptive—entrants into the labor market, we shall have to create at least twelve million new jobs during the next decade—*twice as many* new jobs as we opened up during the unusually prosperous decade from 1947 to 1957.

We must also reckon with the unemployment-creating possibilities inherent in automation. Year by year our productive apparatus becomes more mechanical, more self-regulating, less reliant on human strength or human guidance. As automatic elevators displace elevator men, electronic check sorters displace rows of human check sorters, computers replace billing and inventory clerks, automatic lathes replace lathe operators, the human input required to achieve a given output dwindles. Our total manufacturing production today, for instance, is 20 percent higher than in 1956, but our manufacturing employment is 6 percent *less* than in 1956. And this trend too seems certain to continue, very possibly to intensify, during the 1960s and 1970s. Those who will be displaced by machines may, of course, find employment in other fields. But again, they may not.

How shall we explain this distressing phenomenon of waste, the extravagant non-use of America's wealth? How are we to reconcile it with America's enormous productive power? What is the reason that the inter-action of men and wealth is not proceeding properly?

It is far from easy to determine what the fundamental causes may be—or, indeed, whether what we see is a deeply rooted structural problem of our economy or only a passing phase of difficult adjustment. But whatever the deep-rooted causes, they will not be eliminated overnight. Meanwhile the unemployed press at the employment offices for jobs now. How can we compensate for—if not wholly eliminate—the defects that have impeded us? How can we, through our government, effectively intervene to bring about more production and higher incomes?

ꖯ III

Who Buys
the Nation's Output?

We must begin by looking more closely into the actual process of production itself, into the manner in which the fruitful combination of men and wealth is brought into being.

There is nothing very mysterious to fathom here. If we ask any particular actor on the economic landscape how it happens that he is working (or how it happens that he is not), he will tell us that he works for So-and-so (or that he used to, but has just been laid off); and if we ask So-and-so why he employs this man but not that one, he will tell us that's all it pays for him to employ, there isn't any more demand for his product. Demand is only a term for buying. What the businessman is telling us is that buying gives rise to production and employment—and that not enough buying accounts for nonproduction and unemployment.

But how does this buying itself originate? Who buys the nation's output anyway?

We already know who buys the largest portion of it, for we have seen that the main function of our continuously created new wealth is to replenish the energies of those who created it. In a word, most buying is done by the consumer, who uses his claim on the output he helped to produce to satisfy his needs and desires as best he can. Last year some 58 million consumer units —families or single-dwelling individuals—bought a record $357 billions' worth of food, clothing, gas and oil, plane trips to Florida, electricity, aspirin, and all the other things that go into that enormous grab bag called consumption.

Consumer buying is thus the biggest single source of demand for the businessman, and thus the biggest single source of production and employment. More than three out of every five dollars' worth of production is bought by households. Nevertheless, as these figures themselves make clear, consumers do not buy all of the nation's output. That is perhaps obvious. But what is surprising is the amount by which consumer buying falls short of absorbing the entire final output of the nation. In 1962, out of that total final output of $554 billions—our Gross National Product (GNP for short)—consumers did not buy $197 billions' worth.*

---

* The reader may note the stress on *final* output, and wonder if it is important. It is. Much of the buying of the nation takes place as goods go from one stage of manufacture or processing

Why do not consumers buy more—or even the whole thing?

Three reasons answer the question. First, consumers *cannot* buy the whole output of society because they don't get paid enough wages and salaries and dividends and profits to do so. That is, businessmen, as employers, pay out to their employees less than their businesses take in. And the difference has nothing to do with exploitation or anything like that. The difference is what businesses must *save* to make up for the constant wearing out of productive equipment, plus what they need to provide for additions to real assets, or what they decide to lay aside for safety or liquidity.

We have already seen that as wealth cooperates with labor in the productive process, part of it is worn away, much as a machine will wear down in use. Any business that fails to save up to replace that machine (or buildings or other equipment) is actually consuming its own substance. Hence businesses *must* save, or hold back a portion of their revenues—in part to maintain their assets intact, and in part to provide the wherewithal for the purchase of additional assets, such as new machines,

---

to another, or as they move out from manufacture into the channels of distribution. Thus steel is sold to an automobile manufacturer, and the car (in which the steel is incorporated) is sold to a dealer, and the car at the dealer's (whose price now includes the steel as well as transportation from Detroit and the dealer's expenses) is finally sold to us. To count the steel in the car each time the car was sold would be to include the same output of steel many times instead of once. We avoid this double and triple counting by taking into account only the *final* buying in the economy, the buying that concludes the journey of that particular good or commodity. Consumers are one class of such final buyers. As we shall see, there are three others: foreign buyers, government agencies, and business firms which are adding to their own assets.

more plants, better equipment. Of the $197 billions by which consumer spending fell short of the value of our total final output in 1962, business saving was responsible for $58 billions.

A second reason why households are unable to take up the entire output is perhaps more self-evident. It lies in the fact that after employees and owners receive their incomes from businesses (and just before they metamorphose into consumers) a great hand descends to pluck from their fingers a portion of their incomes. The hand belongs, of course, to the government, and the income it thus snatches away is called taxes.* In 1962 federal income taxes alone took nearly $50 billions out of consumers' hands, while corporate income taxes extracted $23 billions from business treasuries. Add to this the tax receipts of states, counties, cities, townships, etc., and the total amount by which the purchasing potential of consumer and businessman was reduced came to $115 billions.

Here is another obvious cause for the gap between consumer buying and total output. But there is still a third reason to complete the explanation. Despite the fact that the consumer is unable to lay his hands on the income retained by business for its own saving or requisitioned by the government in the form of taxes, he is still well enough off so that he saves a good-sized sum himself. Although not every consumer saves, enough households do save so that consumers as a

---

* Why does government snatch away our income in this predatory and arbitrary way? The answer is very simple, important, and easily forgotten. It is because government *does not sell* its services to us. In part this is due to convention or preference such as the provision of free schooling. In part it is because it is very hard to know how to "sell" police service or the service of the armed forces.

whole actually refrain from using about 7 percent of their disposable incomes. They buy life insurance (which is, of course, a form of saving), put money into the bank, buy new securities, pay back old debts. Personal saving in the United States in 1962 ran to $26 billions.

Add together the $26 billions that consumers save, the $58 billions saved by businesses, the $115 billions of net tax receipts taken by government (including state and local), throw in an adjustment of $2 billions to take care of foreign trade transactions and of Statistical Discrepancies (it is hard to count to a billion accurately), and you account for the large sum of $197 billions of output for which consumers are unable or unwilling to provide demand.

Now the question is, if consumers cannot or will not buy that enormous portion of the nation's output, who will?

In broad outline the answer is evident from our analysis. If consumers are both unable and unwilling to purchase the economy's total output, then if we are to keep production level, much less to increase it, government and business together must be willing to buy up whatever is left.

Business firms, for instance, which have saved part of their incomes for the replacement of old plant and equipment (or the addition of new plant and equipment), must now spend those savings. They will thereby funnel back as market demand the income they held back from their employees and stockholders. It is, of course, a different *kind* of demand—for steel, concrete, machines, rather than for a typical array of consumer goods. But insofar as business spends all its own savings for the regular replacement and expansion of business assets, the economy as a whole automatically gets back a demand for goods equal to the full amounts businesses held back from their employees in the first place.

Similarly, governments—for we are now talking about every level of government from the smallest local unit up—must convert their tax revenues into demand by spending them. This demand, too, will be for a different assortment of commodities and services from those that consumers or businessmen might have ordered. At the local level, government demand typically includes expenditures for schools and teachers' salaries and police and fire and sanitation facilities; at the state level, for roads and state conservation programs and reformatories; and finally, at the federal level, for the manifold activities carried on by the United States Government.

But have we yet made up the "shortfall" in consumer buying? We have seen how business can convert its saving into demand for capital goods and how government can convert its tax revenues into demand for public goods and services. But even if business and government carry out these tasks, there is still one section of demand that is missing. The savings that consumers made—the $26 billions that they did not spend in stores and shops in 1962 because they deposited the money in savings accounts or invested it in new securities or just sat on it—must still be returned to the economy.

Having accounted for the conversion of $115 billions of taxes into government demand, and having shown how the $58 billions of business saving can become investment demand, it seems almost a waste of time to worry about the last $26 billions of savings.

But let us think through the consequences if we do not rescue this last amount of savings too. We have seen that the employers of the nation have laid out a certain sum of wages and salaries and dividends and rents and taxes while they were producing their output. That was their cost and naturally they want to get it back by selling their production. Some of that cost, which was extracted from them (and from their employees) as taxes, they will get back as government demand.* Some will return to them as orders for equipment. But the rest, which they laid out as payments to employees or to themselves, they also expect to get back. To the extent that employees save, however, employers will *not* get it back—at least not in the form of consumer demand: we have already noticed the $26 billions sitting in banks and securities rather than in the cash registers of stores. Unless that last sum of saving is somehow spent for goods and services, there will be large losses for many corporations, sharp cuts in production schedules, layoffs, unemployment, recession. Indeed for 1962, $26 billions were just about equal to total corporate profits after taxes.

Hence it is vital that all consumer saving find a spender, just as all of business' own savings must be spent. To put it differently, when consumers save, they fail to buy. Who will make up for that missing demand? It is clear that we have only two possibilities: government or business (or both).

How can either or both of these sectors perform this

---

* Of course, not every employer enjoys a government contract. Some businesses get much more government demand than others. But then some get the bulk of business or consumer demand. It's the total of all demand that counts.

necessary but baffling feat? *The answer is that they must offset the savings of consumers by making additional expenditures of their own.* In other words, government and business together must spend *more* than they took in through taxes and retained earnings, in order to offset the habits of consumers who spend *less* than they take in. Here is truly the key to understanding the problem of who buys our national output. For the answer is that we cannot buy our entire output unless one sector compensates for another. If consumers save, and government breaks even, then business must spend an *extra* amount to offset those consumer savings. And—to look ahead—if business spending is insufficient to offset the nation's savings, the government must also join the demand-creating process. There is no other way to avoid a business slump.

In Chapter Six, we will learn further about how business—or government—can spend more than its normal receipts without going bankrupt. Meanwhile, if we examine the spending patterns of the major sectors of the economy, this compensatory spending process is clearly visible. Only it is not the government that is the chronic borrower and spender; it is business. In an ordinary year, businesses spend considerably more than their own saving. In fact, they manage to spend all of their own saving plus enough to offset most of the saving of consumers.* The table on page 31 shows this very clearly.

---

* In point of fact, we are seldom able to separate consumer saving from business saving so conveniently as in the text; in real life the two get intermingled. The essential thing is that *all* saving, from whatever source, must be converted into demand—that is, into spending for goods and services.

	Business Saving	Consumer Saving	Total Saving	Business Spending
		(billions of dollars)		
1929	11.5	4.2	15.7	16.2
1940	10.4	4.2	14.6	13.2
1956	43.0	23.0	66.0	67.4
1962	57.9	26.0	83.9	76.2

But note that business did not always succeed in offsetting all the savings that consumers chose to make. This was the case, for instance, in 1940 and in 1962. Who made up the difference? There is only one candidate left: the government.* Those were the years in which the government ran a deficit to supplement the excess of business spending over business saving.

We are getting close to the core of the government deficit spending problem. But before we take that next step, we must pause for a brief but important digression. For our analysis touches here on one of the most profound and fascinating aspects of economics—the process through which economic growth is achieved.

The focus of attention in this book is on the tendency of total demand or total spending in our economy to fall short of our capacity to produce goods and services. The reason it falls short is, of course, because we save —because we choose not to buy everything that is produced. Hence the suggestion arises that saving is somehow bad and should be discouraged. But if saving presents a problem for the economy, this is true only

---

* Technically speaking, there is another candidate: a net favorable foreign trade balance. In ordinary years this picks up $1 billion to $2 billions, and is thus small enough for us safely to ignore.

because we *are* able to produce more than consumers, business, and government are willing to buy.

Many other countries, particularly the poorer, underdeveloped countries, are faced with exactly the opposite problem. There the level of production is so small that consumers must take virtually all of it in order to keep alive, with the result that far too little is left over for the building of factories, production of machines, construction of dams, roads, power plants, schools, research facilities, and all the other vital projects so necessary for a country's development and growth. And, of course, when large military operations and armament production are involved, consumers must tighten their belts so that enough output will be available to feed the engines of war.

The old proverbs about thrift are by no means irrelevant, therefore, under circumstances in which a nation is attempting to build up its productive facilities. Without thrift, no country can add to its capital any more than an individual can add to his. When production is inadequate to satisfy all the demands placed upon it, saving must be encouraged in every possible way. But in the United States in the early 1960s, where demand falls so far short of our capacity to produce, the shoe must be on the other foot. Here the problem is not to add to our capacity but to make full use of it, not to find savings but to make good use of them.

❧ IV

Who Can Buy More?

We have begun to understand the complicated interplay of activity within the economic landscape, to grasp
the way in which an economy generates the demand
to buy back its own product. Yet everything we have
learned thus far has, in a sense, been preliminary to the
questions in which we are ultimately interested: Why
does the economy operate at less than full capacity?
Why do we allow men and machines to stand idle,
while the country cries out for more employment and
more production?

The preceding chapter has given us a way to think
about this problem. If we are to buy everything that
we are capable of producing, we must be sure that all

the saving of the community—business as well as consumer saving—is converted into demand. As we have seen, this can be done only if the business and government sectors spend more than their regular receipts, either by borrowing money, in the case of government, or, in the case of business, by borrowing it or by acquiring it through new stock issues or by drawing on old cash balances. Only in this way can business and government fill up the gap in the demand for goods and services that has been caused by a withdrawal of purchasing power into saving.

All this, however, only goes to explain how a given national output gets bought—or in the case of insufficient business or government "offsets" to saving, how it fails to get bought, with consequent trouble. We have still to solve the problem of how to create *more* demand, how to *increase* our national output, how to *raise* employment. (Only when we are producing as much as we can produce efficiently, need we worry about the problems of too little saving and too much demand.)

But if our preliminary explanations have not directly answered that question, they have surely identified the key to the problem. If we want to increase output, we must increase demand. To increase demand means to increase buying. It follows therefore that if Gross National Product is to rise to its full potential, one of the great buying sectors must lift its purchases. Which one?

Since consumers are the biggest single source of spending, they are a natural first choice as the agent to initiate economic growth. Without any question, if all consumers would spend 10 percent more, the economy would receive a powerful stimulus. Sales of consumer goods would rise, employment would increase in stores and factories making consumer goods, businessmen might well be tempted to spend more on plant and equipment—the economy would boom. The only question is: how do the consumers get the money to buy the extra 10 percent?

One way would be to urge all consumers to save less, to go out and indulge themselves in a spending spree. Such an approach has been tried more than once. It rarely works. For a most persuasive spokesman has already cajoled, begged, even threatened consumers to go out and spend as much as they possibly can—the multibillion-dollar voice of advertising. Hence consumers are probably *already* spending as much as they please or dare. In short, appeals to consumers are apt to be singularly ineffective.

Yet the idea of increasing consumer buying is too good to abandon so easily.* Nor do we have to abandon it. For there is one way in which consumer buying can be rapidly and reliably increased. It is to see that consumers keep their hands on more of the income they get in the first place—*to cut their taxes*. At least $50 billions of potential consumer spending power are sucked up into personal federal income taxes. If tax rates were lowered, some of this income would be left in

---

* The analysis above should make clear the mistaken notions of those who proclaim that "you can't spend yourself into prosperity." Of course you can, so long as we have unemployed resources. In fact, unless spending is rising in some part of the economy, most businessmen will not be willing (or able) to hire additional workers and to produce additional goods and services. The issue of whose spending is to have priority is a different and essentially noneconomic issue, but that has nothing to do with the incontrovertible economic truth that most production and employment are undertaken in response to spending and that demand is just another word for spending.

the individual's pocket; and of each dollar so gained, experience proves that a substantial portion would be quickly spent. A tax cut, in other words, gives us precisely what we want—an immediate stimulus to personal spending, quite independent of any fruitless appeals.

Having worked out the problem for the consumer, we should find no difficulty in applying the same solution to the businessman. Like the consumer, the businessman is unlikely to respond vigorously to mere oratory urging him to spend more of his business saving or of consumer saving. Presumably, businessmen are already spending as much for plant and equipment or for commercial and residential construction as they find it profitable and think it prudent to do.

To be sure, many corporations would like to step up their pace of expansion. Most large firms have plans for expansion on the shelf, awaiting a propitious moment. But the propitious moment will have to be announced by something more substantial than exhortation. Indeed, the disappointingly slow growth in the demand for goods and services in recent years has left such a burdensome and worrisome surplus of idle productive capacity in its wake, that management today is more cautious than venturesome in its outlook. Thus while appeals to undertake additional investment may move the businessman insofar as he understands economics, they are hardly likely to move him insofar as he understands business.

A much more likely way to persuade businessmen to act is to increase their profits. And this is where a tax cut can play a role similar to the one that it plays in increasing the spendable income of a consumer. Federal taxes on corporation profits amount to nearly $25 billions. A decrease here can also quickly release spending power to swell national demand.

Yet the case is not precisely the same as with the consumer. When we cut taxes on ordinary households we can be fairly certain that the windfall will be used to buy goods and services for the household: steadily rising trends of consumer spending and borrowing show that the pressure for higher living standards has been built into the very character structure of the average American. But we cannot be so unequivocally sure about the fate of the larger profits resulting from a cut in business taxes. They *might* be paid out in higher wages, salaries, or dividends—and thus go to increase consumer demand—or they *might* be used to buy more equipment, which was the immediate purpose of the tax cut. On the other hand, they also *might* simply be left idle within the business, adding to business liquidity rather than to business buying.

But there is also a last and best possibility. It is that the tax cut might act as a kind of galvanic stimulus to business, causing it to revise its whole future profit expectations upward and to embark on a substantially raised program of building and expansion. The real promise of a tax cut for business is that it might lead business to spend more—even much more—than the tax cut itself. The hope is that a tax cut would induce businessmen to start a major investment program that would put to use all of the otherwise unused savings in the community.

Will a tax cut have this electrifying effect? Or will it merely be saved or only partially spent by business?

There is no more important practical question in economics, and none more difficult to answer. The motives behind business investment have been intensively studied, but they remain elusive and obscure. Many factors bear on the final decision to invest or not to invest: the current rate of profit on sales, the presence or absence of exciting technological possibilities, the rate of change in sales or orders, the cost of funds, the extent of international tension, the domestic political situation, personal motives of vanity, caution, daring, rivalry, and, perhaps most important, the degree of excess plant capacity.

Hence, in the end, the effect of a tax cut on business spending is always uncertain. Most economists have come to hold a considerable respect for the inherent élan, the expansive push, of business enterprise, and they believe that, when capacity utilization is high, business will step up its investments (although by exactly how much is always open to question). At the same time, however, it is clear enough that the combined demands of consumers and government *must* remain at least on an even keel if business is to turn a tax cut into an investment push. After all, the rate of profit on an idle machine is zero. This means that the chances of viewing a tax cut as the long awaited "propitious moment" are considerably enhanced if business sales do not decline together with taxes.

Why should they? This brings us back to the role that the federal budget plays in the national economic picture. Now we can begin to see that the budget has a major significance in the very terms we have just been discussing—holding the general state of business on an even keel. For it should now be evident that if a tax cut is matched by a cut in government spending, total sales may very well fall. Certainly the tax cut will fail to boost total demand in that case. Instead, it will simply *decrease* government demand by the same amount by which it increases consumer or business demand.

The point is so important that we must spell it out with figures. In 1962, for example, the major sources of demand for our Gross National Product were as follows:

	($ billions)
Consumer demand	357
Business demand for investment goods and construction	77
Federal, local, and state government demand	115
Foreign demand, and statistical discrepancy	5
TOTAL DEMAND	554

Now let us suppose that as a result of a tax cut of $10 billions, consumer and business demand were each to rise by $5 billions, while at the same time government spending were trimmed by $10 billions to match its lower tax receipts. The demand for Gross National Product would then look like this:

	($ billions)	Change in Demand ($ billions)
Consumer demand	362	+ 5
Business demand	82	+ 5
Government demand	105	−10
Foreign demand, etc.	5	0
TOTAL DEMAND	554	0

In other words, we have gained nothing. As a matter of fact, since consumers will actually save *some* of their new-found incomes—even if only five cents on the dollar—the increase in consumer demand would be less than the $5 billions we have shown. Thus there would be a slight *fall* in total demand unless business spent all its tax savings *and then some more*. It is impossible to predict dogmatically what business might in fact do in such circumstances. But in the face of falling government demand—of slack aircraft production schedules in Long Island, or cutbacks in orders to electronic plants in Los Angeles, or large-scale dismissals of federal office help in Philadelphia or New York—there is at least a strong possibility that business would not embark on a major investment drive, but would tend to increase its investments only cautiously and might even decrease them.

Is there no way out of this dilemma? It must be clear by now that there is a very simple way out. It is to increase consumer and business demand and *not to decrease government demand*.

And how do we do this? Obviously by cutting taxes and *not* cutting government spending. To go back to our previous example, suppose we again cut taxes on consumers by $5 billions and taxes on business by $5 billions, but this time keep government spending unchanged. The result is as simple as a problem in elementary arithmetic:

	($ *billions*)	Change in Demand ($ *billions*)
Consumer demand	362	+ 5
Business demand	82	+ 5
Government demand	115	0
Foreign demand, etc.	5	0
TOTAL DEMAND	564	+10

We have raised the demand for Gross National Product by $10 billions—the amount of the tax cut. And now, with no cutback in the Long Island aircraft plants, no layoffs in Los Angeles or Philadelphia, there is more reason to hope that business *will* launch a large-scale investment effort that could raise Gross National Product still more.

We have found a solution to the problem of how to increase demand.* By cutting taxes and maintaining the level of government spending, or by directly increasing spending without raising taxes by an equivalent amount, we can insure that total demand will go up, production up, employment up, incomes up. In fact the only problem is that something else will also go up: the deficit. To be precise, it will go up $10 billions.

Thus we have finally entered the icy waters of deficit financing. We have reached the threshold of the key problem we set out to investigate.

Before we take the chilly plunge however, let us stop to reflect on two points. First, it must already be clear that the government budget is an instrument to secure the balance of the entire economy. It is, or can be, a means of assuring that total demand is large enough to provide reasonably full employment; a means of assuring that all the nation's savings are converted into buying.

* It is worth noting that there are really two ways of increasing demand. One is the tax cut method (with government spending held steady) explained above. The other is to keep taxes steady but to increase government spending. The advantage of the tax cut route is that it is *quicker*, and it allows the private economy to spend the "booster" as it wishes. The advantage of the increased government spending route is that it is *surer*, and it allows the added demand to be directly channeled into those areas and purposes that public policy selects. Or, of course, the two methods can be used in combination.

Second, it must also be clear that the government budget is in essence no different from the "budget" of the entire business sector or of the consumer sector. They too have their demand-making uses. They too create savings, or in the case of the business sector convert saving into demand. The only difference is that the government deficit or surplus is *controllable*, while the budget of the entire business sector or of the consumer sector is not. If the American economic system made it possible to manipulate business decisions by *force majeure*—now forcing businessmen to invest, now prohibiting them from doing so, now making sure that consumers did little or no saving, now insuring that they saved heavily—we would not need to use the government budget as a balance wheel, as an instrument of control. But such iron-clad manipulation of the activities of the private sectors would, of course, mean a radical redesign of the private enterprise system. It would probably mean the end of capitalism. Thus it is important to recognize that the government budget is the implement of economic control which interferes least with the freedom of private economic activity that we wish to preserve.

V

Spending and Borrowing

Thus we have come to see that a government deficit is essentially a way of raising demand. Yet the very thought of a government "creating demand" by borrowing people's savings and spending them—"squandering them" is the phrase that comes all too readily to mind—is not one to give us peace of mind. Now the noneconomist, who has thus far been patiently following this exposition, suddenly digs in his heels. It is one thing, he tells himself, to create demand, but how is one to cope with the debt that keeps piling up as a consequence?

It is understandable that the process of borrowing and

spending should raise just such kinds of objections, for it is here that the view from sea level and from the economist's vantage point differ most sharply. And yet if we can persuade the noneconomist to take just one more look from his unaccustomed perspective, we may get him to see a surprising thing. It is that the process of borrowing and spending—of "deficit financing"—is by no means limited to the government. On the contrary, it is equally or even more conspicuous in the consumer and business sectors.

Look at consumers first. On balance, as we have noted, our consumer households are savers—to the amount of $26 billions in 1962. But now if we look more closely at these households we can see that they are also borrowers and spenders, and that year by year the total of their debts—and assets—increases. In 1962, for instance, consumers paid for $4 billions of their purchases of automobiles and household appliances through the use of installment borrowing, and, when we include personal loans and the purchase of homes through mortgage borrowing, we find that consumers spent $21 billions of borrowed money.* And there was nothing exceptional about 1962: over the preceding ten years, consumer debt outstanding, including mortgage

---

* Most new houses are originally built by a contractor who has borrowed the necessary funds from a bank. That is why residential construction is conventionally included in the total for business investment spending, which is where we have included it in our analysis of the spending patterns of the major sectors of the economy. After a builder has done the initial borrowing and spent that money on the construction of the house, however, the home buyer comes along and takes the house off his hands, paying for most of it with a mortgage that replaces the construction loan. Thus a debt originally contracted in the business sector is shifted into the consumer sector.

debt, had been rising at an average annual rate of $19 billions.

The same general pattern is visible in the business sector, where we see the same regular borrowing and spending as in the consumer world. In every normal year, businessmen have to go to the public or to the money markets to gather up additional funds—not, of course, funds to pay for their ordinary running expenses, but to pay for the big capital items, the new investments, the additional plant and equipment that cannot be covered in a regular business budget.

Thus the realization that is forced on us is that borrowing and spending are indispensable parts of demand creation within the private as well as the public sector. When the government borrows and spends, we call it "deficit financing," but the essential process of spending more than one's regular income is as characteristic of the consumer or the business firm as it is of the government.

The realization is at first a curious one, and one that again emphasizes the difference between the individual and the economy. Find an individual who is steadily accumulating debt, and you have probably found one who is in trouble; find one who is paying off his debts, and you have probably found one in good economic health. But find a nation whose domestic debts are mounting, whose mortgages year by year are increasing, whose corporate debentures are proliferating, whose local and state and federal bond issues are growing, and the chances are that you have found a nation whose rate of growth is high, whose economy is buoyant, whose savings are abundant, whose business is booming.

On the other hand, find a nation whose domestic debts are static or declining, and the likelihood is very great that you have found one whose fortunes are in decline.

Look, for instance, at the period from 1930 to 1935, when the United States economy went through the longest and most damaging decline of its history. In the earlier year, net corporate debt had totaled $89 billions; by 1935 it was down to $75 billions. Net consumer debt, which amounted to $59 billions in 1935, fell to $41 billions five years later. Net state and local debt increased only from $14 to $16 billions over the period. Only federal debt went against the trend—from $17 billions to $34 billions—but the rise in federal debt was not enough to offset the decline elsewhere. Total debt in the economy shrank over the period by about 8 percent.

Did this decline in debt mean that companies, individuals, and local governments were in healthy condition? It did not. It showed that businesses were failing, that individuals were unable to buy houses or durable goods, that road and school construction had come to a virtual halt. Contrast the situation between 1950 and 1955. Now net state and local debts climbed from $21 billions to $38 billions, corporate debts mounted from $251 billions to $403 billions, individual indebtedness from $97 billions to $172 billions, and federal debt rose slightly, from $219 billions to $232 billions. Did this mean that municipalities and corporations and households were in weaker financial shape in 1955 than in 1950? On the contrary, every index of well-being was at a record high.

Thus, as a nation's private and public debts go, so goes its health. In the sharpest possible contrast to the case of the single individual, a national economy welcomes debt, thrives on it, and grows strong with it.*

What is the explanation of this perplexing fact? What is it about debt that makes it a source of potential weakness when viewed from one angle and a source of potential strength when viewed from another?

The answer is less perplexing than it might appear to be at first glance. In the first place, we have already seen that what makes businessmen willing to produce goods and services is demand—spending by customers. Because money is borrowed to be spent, rising debts are the counterpart to rising demand and spending, which in turn leads to expanding output and employment. This is central to the entire subject and will occupy a great deal of our attention in later pages.

Meanwhile, however, there is a second and equally important aspect to the question of how debt can take on a different appearance, depending upon the standpoint from which we look at it. A debt is a claim. The person who *owes* the claim obviously counts it as a subtraction from his net worth. But the person who *owns* the claim, the creditor, counts it as an addition to *his* net worth.

Does this mean that owner and ower cancel each other and that debts are essentially meaningless? Hardly. Both owner and ower feel that their commonly shared debt is backed by something. What is that something?

It is an asset. The most common purpose for which

---

* In all fairness, this statement should of course be qualified to exclude nations who use debt creation to finance demands far in excess of their capacity to produce and to create wealth.

a debt is contracted is to enable the debtor to acquire the use of wealth. Thus a consumer borrows money to buy a car, or a house; or a company borrows money to buy a plant or a new building.*

All debts are not incurred to acquire assets, of course. A man may incur a debt because he is a spendthrift or a company may incur a debt because it is running at a loss. In such cases, the claims of whoever is brave enough to lend money are basically "backed" by the future earning power of the borrower. The trusting friend or the lending bank believes, rightly or wrongly, that the friend can change his ways or the company can turn a corner, and that future income will allow the debt to be repaid.

Asset-acquiring debts have a very different significance from the debts on "current account" of a business that is failing to meet ordinary expenses or a household that simply cannot meet its bills. For behind the first kind of claim there is an increase in ownership of real property, real goods. Thus behind the mounting volume of mortgage indebtedness is a mounting body of real buildings, behind the rising total of installment debt a rising agglomeration of autos and refrigerators and other durable goods, behind the expanding volume of corporate debt an expanding stock of plant and equipment, ma-

---

* Not all assets are acquired in this way, of course. A man may save up and buy a car out of his accumulated savings and incur no debt. A business may finance expansion out of its past savings or by selling stock and thus enlarging its ownership equity. But debt is a very common and useful means of acquiring assets. It is a kind of halfway house on the road to equity ownership, for frequently a debt will be gradually repaid and an asset will then become owned outright. Or as we can now see, the claim against that asset would then pass from the lender to the borrower, who is now "in the clear."

chinery, buildings, inventories. Hence if a nation with growing debts is typically becoming richer, the reason is obvious. It is accumulating real wealth.

And what about government debts? Are they debts contracted just because the government is a careless budgeter, or debts contracted because the government is also an accumulator of wealth? It is clear, of course, that the government *does* create and does own real wealth. The most recent estimated value of government buildings alone in the United States, for example, was $168 billions in 1958. And this does not begin to itemize the real wealth that has been created by government spending. What of the government's share in the value of the nation's airports, what of the housing projects, the conservation programs, the enormous power plants, the atomic energy installations, the space exploration laboratories and equipment, the cyclotrons, the ships and planes and vehicles, the hospitals, the stocks of metals and food, the power lines for rural electrification, the research facilities?

These are some of the assets "behind" our national debt. If these evidences of wealth were owned by a business, it would be considered only proper to "capitalize" them as assets. Why then do we not regard government debt as the other side of the coin of public wealth-creation?

The answer lies largely in the convention of bookkeeping. Businesses have long differentiated between spending for current purposes and spending for capital purposes, and they carefully distinguish between debts incurred for one purpose and debts incurred for another. When in a normal year a business spends $1 million more than its net income on plant expansion, it does not report a million-dollar loss to its stockholders. Not so with the government. When the government spends a million dollars to build a hospital or a hundred million dollars to build an aircraft carrier, the money it spends is considered to be on "current" account, just as if it had been spent for the regular payroll or maintenance of a government department.

Many countries—including Sweden and Great Britain—separate their public wealth-creation from their expenditures on "current account"—a practice that obviously goes a long way toward quieting fears of growing debt. For it is then legitimate to talk, not just of "increasing the national debt," but also of "increasing the national wealth." Perhaps some day we will make this sensible change. But in the meantime we can at least understand that the process of debt-creation is no less conducive to wealth-creation in the public sector than in the private.

Needless to say, however, deficit spending *need* not create wealth unless the spending is for wealth-creating purposes. The government can spend its borrowed money for foolish as well as for wise purposes, for ephemeral as well as for lasting objects. But so, of course, can the private spenders of borrowed funds. And one more thought. It may be objected that business properly capitalizes its assets because they are earning assets, whereas the government properly does not, because its assets do not "earn" an income. We have already noted that this reflects the fact that the government does not sell its services, but taxes the whole nation for them. But insofar as government wealth increases the income of the nation—and who could deny the income-creating power of our vast road system, school system, dams, conservation projects, research facilities, etc.?—it *does* increase the government's tax revenues and therefore *is* an earning asset.

The subject of debt becomes much less disturbing when we think of its counterpart in assets. And yet second thoughts show us that our reassurance is not quite so solidly based as it might appear at first. After all, a consumer can use his borrowings to buy an excellent asset—say a new car—and yet that consumer may go bankrupt because he cannot pay his debt back. So can a corporation go bankrupt, even though it has bought good earning assets with its debt. Hence the presence of assets, no matter how comforting as a reminder that debts are claims against wealth, does not put to rest all our suspicions about debt. The important questions yet remain: How much can a borrower afford to borrow? And does he not have to pay his debt back?

It may help us to get to the bottom of the debt problem if we start with the kind of debt that is closest to home: consumer debt. How much can we, as householders, borrow? When do we repay our debts?

No one person can tell another precisely how much debt the other can carry. But we know the principle that is involved in coming to a sensible answer. A man, or a household, can carry as much debt as he can afford to "service"—that is, as much as he can afford to pay in the way of interest and amortization. The amount naturally varies from man to man. But the idea is simple enough. A consumer can borrow up to the point at which some lender thinks the risk of not getting paid interest and amortization is too great to warrant making a loan.

How about paying the debt back? Assuredly each consumer recognizes the need to pay his debt back, unless he is to declare himself bankrupt or to lose possession of the asset he bought with the loan or to see his credit standing fall.

But that is not quite all. For what is true of each and every consumer is not true of all of them together. As household A finishes paying for its car, household B begins paying for its. As X pays off his charge account bill or installment loan, Y is just charging something on his account or taking out a new loan. The fact that consumer debt as a whole goes steadily upward shows that *consumers as a whole do not pay off their debts*.

To repeat, it is obvious that *individually* consumers must and do repay their debts. But *collectively* they need not and do not. In the consumer "sector" total debt rises steadily, a fact that appears less alarming when we remember that it is only an indication that consumer-owned wealth is also rising and that, by spending more, consumers are creating more jobs and more incomes for one another.

Nothing so distresses the noneconomist as this first glimpse of the endless process of debt-creation. There must be an end to it, he insists. Sooner or later the paper house must fall, the "grim reckoning" must come. Yet there is no reason why the house of paper should fall, so long as it is only the obverse of a house of real wealth. So long as wealth increases, debts (or equities) must also increase. To be sure, in the dim distant future when every household has as much real wealth as it wishes, when our population is static and our economy no longer geared to growth, then the process of debt-expansion will stop. But until that happy day of satiation is reached we must expect—and wish for—the amount of debt to grow.

We have lingered over consumer debt, but the case gets even more interesting and significant when we turn to business debts. Of course, business as a whole acts as consumers do. Individual businesses contract debts and repay them, but the total of business debt continues to grow, as we have previously seen. *Like consumers, business collectively does not pay back its debt* —and for the same reason. Business debt, like consumer debt, piles up as its assets pile up.

But now let us look at the *individual* business. Does it always pay back its debts? Surprisingly, the answer is no, it does not. Take two of the world's most successful businesses, American Telephone and Telegraph and Consolidated Edison Company of New York, and look at their debt totals:

	Total Debt Outstanding	
	A.T.&T.	Consolidated Edison
1929	$1,148,000,000	$240,000,000
1962	8,382,000,000	1,439,000,000

This does not mean, it need hardly be said, that A.T.&T. and Consolidated Edison default on their debts. When each bond comes due, it is scrupulously honored and each bondholder is repaid in full. But A.T.&T. and Consolidated Edison do not pay back their bonds by drawing down company cash. Instead they float a new issue of bonds and with the proceeds from these pay off the old issue. This procedure, called "refunding," is a standard business practice: since 1945, A.T.&T. and its subsidiaries have refunded $252 millions of debt, or nearly a quarter of what they owed in 1945.

Can an individual business carry its debts forever, *never* paying them back? If its earning power remains high enough to cover the interest payments and if the bond-buying public continues to trust in its future prospects, there is no reason why a corporation debt cannot be carried indefinitely. There is no prospect of A.T.&T. or Consolidated Edison (or any number of other utility or manufacturing companies) repaying their debts in the foreseeable future—a fact that in no wise weakens public confidence in these well-managed companies.

And this brings us finally to the biggest "company" of all, the Government of the United States. We have reached the all-important questions: How much can the federal government borrow? When must it repay its debts? But these are such important matters that we must give them a chapter to themselves.

❧ VI

Government Debts

Can we think about the problem of government borrowing as if the United States Government were in fact a gigantic business? The image may help us comprehend certain aspects of spending and borrowing, but we must realize how enormously more powerful the government is than any business, of no matter what size.

A business—even a legal monopoly like A.T.&T.— is never *sure* of its income. A sudden change in people's habits, or a startling invention, such as a wrist radio, could seriously damage A.T.&T.'s income overnight. In other words, it is always conceivable that any business will not be able to enjoy its income, and will therefore be unable to take care of the interest on its debt.

Can this happen to a national government? We have but to think the problem through to see the difference —a difference of kind and not merely of degree—that separates governmental economic power and business economic power. A business obtains its income by selling its wares—that is, by *persuading* some people to give it a part of their incomes. A government derives its income by taxing people—that is by levying a *compulsory* charge on their incomes, property, or purchases. Hence as long as the government retains the sovereign power to tax, it can always depend on receiving the income it needs to pay its interest.

Whether or not this would be inflationary is a matter we shall take up in due course. Meanwhile, however, the sheer economic power of the federal government explains why the credit rating of the government is the most solid in the economy and why a government bond is regarded as being virtually without risk of default. It also helps us realize that the assets "behind" government bonds are of an entirely different order of strength from those "behind" the best corporate bonds. To be sure, as we have seen, there are public buildings, roads, land, vessels that have been bought out of public borrowing, and that are comparable to similar assets created through debt in the private sector. But there is something else behind the public debt that can never be duplicated in the private part of the economy. *This is the power to tax, the power to legislate, the power to create currency.*

Nonetheless, even the impressive picture of a government armed with the power of the tax collector and the printing press still does not bring out the crucial difference between public and private debts. There have been, after all, businesses (such as private banks before the days of the Federal Reserve System) that printed their own notes, and a local utility is nearly as effective as a government in securing a captive source of income. Yet even such businesses cannot enjoy one final and all-important advantage that comes of being a nation: they cannot owe their debts to themselves.

For every business, even A.T.&T., must face creditors *outside of itself* who could, were worst to come to worst, take over the business. But this is not true of government. Its creditors are themselves part of the enterprise called the United States. It is the people of the United States who are both the lenders and the borrowers, the people of the United States from whom the government extracts taxes and to whom it also pays interest. Thus the government debt is an internal debt, *a debt that members of a community owe to one another.*

This point is of such importance that we must take a moment or two to make it crystal clear. Let us first imagine two country clubs that decide to embark on building programs at the same time. One club, which we will call the Business Club, finances its new buildings by borrowing from a bank; the other club, the Government Club, finances its new buildings by borrowing from its own members. Now each builds identical facilities costing identical amounts. Does this mean that the clubs are in identical financial shape?

By no means. The Business Club owes its loan to a bank and each quarter when the interest comes due its directors hold a nervous meeting. They must be sure that the membership has paid up its dues, for they know that if they fail to meet the interest payments the bank will take over the club. Not so with the Govern-

ment Club. Here the directors hold their quarterly meet-
ings in an atmosphere of quiet composure, for they
know that they can always meet the interest payments.
Why? Because they can always assess their members
in case dues fall short. And how do we know that their
members can be assessed? Because they would be paying those assessments right back to the members in
the form of interest on the bonds the members hold.

Take another example, a fanciful one. Let us imagine
that our government debt is equally distributed among
all families and that all families are taxed alike. How
big could such a debt be, without fear of failure to meet
the interest? The answer is Infinitely Big. Suppose that
each family owned $1,000,000 worth of bonds on which
it received an annual interest of $25,000. There would
be no trouble in paying the interest. The government
would tax each family $25,000 and then immediately
turn around and pay each family $25,000 in interest. No
one would be better or worse off, and a debt of gigantic
size could be effortlessly serviced.

Indeed, it is the fact that the government debt is *not*
equally distributed which sets practical limits on its size.
Obviously some people are taxed more heavily than they
are recompensed by interest, and others receive more
interest than they pay in taxes. A big government debt
may therefore involve problems of income redistribution
from the tax-paying to the bond-holding members of
the community. This may pose problems against an in-
definite expansion of the debt, but these are not the
problems we hear about. And in any case, because the
United States Government debt is so much more widely
held than in the 1930s, it could be vastly larger before

the political strains of redistribution would become burdensome.

Thus a government that borrows internally can always meet its obligations.* Can it pay back its debt? Of course—in exactly the same way as a business. When each bond comes due it will be fully paid off by the proceeds of the sale of a new bond. Like a great business, a government need never pay back its debts—a fact that we can again make less psychologically disturbing by picturing those debts as claims on public assets.

Nevertheless it all has a very suspicious ring. There is something about the "we owe it to ourselves" argument that sounds too good to be true. There is a lingering feeling that even if we do owe it to ourselves, we will nonetheless have to pay the debt back some day.

Well, let us suppose that we do decide to pay the debt back in order to lift its "burden" from our children's backs. We shall return later to the problem of how the government gets the money to pay back the debt, but for the moment let us simply imagine that it announces that all government bonds will be paid off in full at the nearest post office.

Next we will suppose that you have $5,000 worth of government bonds that you had previously set aside to

---

* Note that a government that borrows externally (from another country)—as was the case with England during World War II—is not always able to service its debt. England could collect the interest easily enough in pounds, but she owed it in *dollars*. This led to severe trouble and to a forced devaluation of the pound. Hence an externally-held national debt is an entirely different matter from an internally-held one. It can indeed result in default. However, only about 5 percent of the United States debt is externally-owed.

give to your children—meanwhile enjoying the interest you received. You would obediently take your bond to your post office and emerge with a check for $5,000, which you could then deposit in your bank.

Question: have you gained? You have lost a bond generally regarded as the single best credit risk in the world and you now hold cash instead. If you want to enjoy an income, you will now have to find some other obligation to invest in. If you want to hold cash, you will have to forgo the interest you formerly had.

But your children—are they not better off? They are rid of a $5,000 asset that they were once going to inherit, and in exchange they will inherit $5,000 in cash, or in some other, slightly less iron-clad security. It is hard to say that they are any better off.

Well, you will say, at least the government has gained. It no longer owes a debt of $5,000. This is true, but what did it cost the government to owe that debt? The interest, as we have seen, was a minor problem, for it merely taxed Peter to pay Paul, or sometimes Peter to pay Peter. The face value of the debt was no trouble since it could be refunded when it was due. It is true the government now has no debt to worry about, but since there was little worry in the first place, the gain seems small.

For many citizens, though, the government's "gain," such as it is, is overshadowed by a considerable loss. Government bonds, being as near to cash as a security can be and yet pay the holder a reward (interest), serve an extremely useful purpose. Commercial banks and corporations regularly hold vast quantities of government bonds as earning assets that can be converted into cash, without risk of loss, at a moment's notice.

Many millions of small investors who want a good return and a very safe security turn naturally to government as a proper place for their savings. Now that the government debt is paid back, these banks and investors must choose the next best thing. But no security —not even A.T.&T.—is as good as the government's promise to pay.

But we have forgotten the problem of how the government is going to pay back its debt—that is, where it is going to get the money to give you that $5,000 check. Suppose we decided to pay back the debt at the rate of $10 billions a year, so that in about thirty years we would have paid it all off. How would the government get that $10 billions a year? Unless you would like the government to print the money, it will have to get it through taxes. Clearly that would entail some of us being taxed $10 billions extra in order to pay some others of us that very same $10 billions: Peter would have handed his money, with a detour through Washington, to Paul—or to himself. In the process, engraved certificates of debt would have been canceled. Thereafter, Peter would no longer pay the taxes needed to pay interest on $10 billions of those debt certificates. But then Paul would no longer get his U.S. Treasury checks. Would the country be better off?

To take the matter a step further, suppose that all the corporations in the nation paid off *their* debts. Now clearly for the corporations, which owe external debts— that is, debts outside the family—this would be a net gain of a sort. Of course, they would have had to part with cash that they might have used for other purposes. But would it be a gain for the country at large? People who had previously counted their A.T.&T. and Consolidated Edison bonds among their soundest assets would now have no such valuable pieces of paper: they would have no promises to pay from any business. They could, of course, invest directly as owners in the business—in stocks. But for the millions of investors who do not want stocks—or for the banks and life insurance companies who wish to protect our money by buying bonds, the disappearance of debt would mean a serious loss.

Is it true then that the government need never repay its internally-held debts? Yes, it is true. Is this perfectly safe? Yes, it is perfectly safe. Is it not a trick, a sleight-of-hand, a kind of financial fraud? No, it is none of these.

But it is one thing to declare this, or even to work it through, and another thing to believe it without a lingering sense of doubt. In the end perhaps there is only one way to rid oneself, once and for all, of these very understandable fears. It is once again to mount to the economist's perch and to survey the national wealth that underlies the bonds (or the shares of stock) that concern us so.

For then we see again that wealth consists of the natural and man-made productive potential of our country and of the actual use that is made of that potential. The paper—the bonds, stocks, mortgages, notes that clutter up our safe deposit boxes; even the money that is in our wallets—is *not* that wealth. It merely establishes our claims against wealth. In the case of business bonds or of mortgages or of promissory notes, it establishes that Company X owes to Person Y certain payments for so many years, during which time Y has a lien against such-and-such a piece of property or equipment belonging to X or against X's assets in general. Or it says that Person Z owes to Bank Q so and so many regular payments, in default of which Bank Q will possess Person Z's property or garnishee his salary. None of these claims makes or unmakes wealth. It establishes legal rights and obligations on it.

The government does not, by a convention of accounting, issue its bonds against stated assets, as a company might. As a result, the holder of $10,000 worth of Series H Savings Bonds or of $100,000 worth of Treasury 2½s of 1972 does not have a lien on a PT boat or on a section of U.S. Highway 914 or of a veteran's hospital or a housing project. He might feel better if he did, but it would make no real difference. For what the bonds really promise us is that we have a claim on the Treasury of the Government of the United States for so-and-so many years for interest, and thereafter for the face value of the bond. We will get the interest paid to us, not only because the full power of the government is prepared to see to it that its obligation is honored, but because the very same national community will be both paying the taxes which pay for the interest, *and* receiving those taxes back again *as* interest. And finally, we will all get our money back when our bond has matured because the government will sell new bonds to replace the old ones.

What does all this strange process of claim and payment look like from the economist's perch? He sees in it two aspects different from those that usually appear to us. First, he sees that the process allows us to exchange our claims, and to acquire the particular claims suitable to our needs and temperaments. The presence of bonds and stocks makes possible a *market* for capital, a market of great convenience for us and of huge benefit to the economy.

Second, he sees as well that the process of acquiring claims—government claims as well as private claims—is essentially a process of creating demand, of transmuting idle savings into active spending. In the process of transmuting these savings into demand, assets are usually created, for typically the reason that savings are borrowed by individuals and companies is to bring a new asset into existence or to acquire one. Much government borrowing could be viewed as asset-creation if we operated the government's books that way. But it matters not. Government borrowing is demand-creating, whether or not it is ticketed against asset-creating expenditure or merely against office pay. It is perhaps a curious way of arranging things, but if the process of business demand-creation is insufficient, there is no other way to avoid unemployment.

❧ VII

Inflation

But is it not all inflationary? That is what one constantly hears. Won't deficit financing lead to a sky-rocketing cost of living, so that we may all have more dollars but won't be able to buy as much with them as before?

The fear of inflation is one of the greatest obstacles to a rational understanding of the mechanics of government finance. Since disastrous price inflations have occurred with distressing frequency in the history of civilized man, the fear is not to be dismissed casually.

But let us begin by making a very important distinction. None of the really sensational inflations—the inflation that followed our own American Revolution, that came during the French Revolution, that contributed to the downfall of the Southern Confederacy during the Civil War, that demoralized Germany after World War I, or that plagued the European countries and China after World War II—can be attributed solely to government spending as such. Essentially they all stemmed from the holocaust of war, from the wholesale destruction of productive capacity, and from the breakdown of the government's ability to organize and direct the affairs of the nation. Similarly, the galloping inflations in the underdeveloped lands, such as Brazil, are the outcome of the peculiar strains and stresses of seeking to expand too rapidly an economy that rests on an inadequate productive base of roads, factories, power plants, etc.

All the truly disastrous inflations, in other words, are ascribable to inadequate or damaged *productive* capacity. It is certainly imaginable that if we should suffer a war catastrophe similar to those we have mentioned, we too might experience a nightmare inflation.

This is not the kind of inflation with which Americans are concerned. When we think of inflation, we think of the more or less steady rise in prices that has afflicted the economy ever since the guns stopped firing at the end of World War II.* Hence the first question

---

* It is not true, as many people believe, that inflation has gone on almost uninterruptedly in America. Since 1800, the rise in wholesale prices has been at an annual rate of less than 1 percent, and almost all the price increases that have been marked up over this period were associated with the Napoleonic Wars, the Civil War, and the two world wars. In fact, prices have declined in more than forty of the past ninety years. Although prices today are about double the 1929 level, they are actually only one-third higher than they were in 1920.

we must examine is whether that inflation is traceable to deficit financing.

The chart on page 68 shows this is not the case. Here we see, year by year, changes in the cost of living (the white rectangles) compared with the deficits (the striped rectangles). The chart shows absolutely no systematic relationship between government deficits and changes in the price level. Note, for example, how prices rose even with federal *surpluses* in 1946-48, 1950-51, 1956-57, and 1960. On the other hand, prices fell in 1949 even though the government ran at a deficit. Large deficits in 1953 and 1954 were accompanied by modest upward movements in prices. The large deficit in 1958 resulted in a price rise that was smaller than in the surplus year of 1957. This pattern is entirely contrary to the widely held opinion that large deficits cause large upward price movements, and that prices tend to decline or to remain stable when the government spends less than it takes in in taxes.

This is nothing new in our history. For example, during the years 1897 to 1913, this country experienced an unusually sharp degree of peacetime inflation; prices rose 50 percent over the period. This was twice as fast as the rise in prices from 1948 to 1962. Yet the federal government ran a *surplus* in seven of the sixteen years from 1897 to 1913, and the national debt at the end of the period was 3 percent *lower* than it had been at the beginning.*

---

* It is also interesting to note that the United States was on the traditional gold standard and permitted free convertibility of dollars into gold for all holders during most of this period. In other words, even the gold standard in its classic form, the most conservative of monetary techniques, was no guarantee that inflation could be avoided.

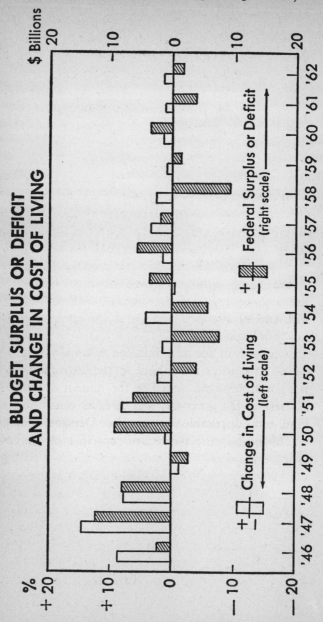

BUDGET SURPLUS OR DEFICIT
AND CHANGE IN COST OF LIVING

What all of this is meant to show is that inflation cannot be linked, in a purely mechanical fashion, to government deficits. Instead we must always look behind the symptom of rising prices to the *real* forces at work.

And what are they? As every freshman economics student knows, the answer is Supply and Demand. In other words, when prices are rising, it is because Demand is outpacing Supply—either forcing prices up or making it possible for sellers to raise their prices—and when prices again fall, it is because Supply has caught up with Demand. When customers are bidding actively for goods, when order backlogs are rising sharply, most businessmen will take advantage of the situation to raise prices. But when production schedules have been increased and additional quantities of goods and services come onto the market, then the apparent shortages will tend to disappear and prices will either rise more slowly or begin to fall.

Now we can see why inflation is usually linked so closely to wartime conditions. As the huge demands of the government are added to the normal demands of the rest of the economy, and as taxes usually lag behind, total disposable incomes rise: Demand goes way up. Meanwhile the productive capacities of the economy are strained to the limit, largely turning out things that contribute nothing to the purchasable needs and desires of the citizens of the country: consumer supply holds steady or actually shrinks. Demand and Supply thus get hopelessly out of touch with each other, and the inflationary spiral begins to twist.

This shows, too, why government deficits *can* indeed lead to price inflation. We have already seen that the government can add to the purchasing power of the country. A deficit, in other words, means that the demand for the country's production will be bigger than if the government's budget were balanced or running a surplus. Since an increase in Demand without a corresponding increase in Supply will lead to higher prices, deficit spending by the government can—under certain conditions—lead to inflation.

But those certain conditions are crucial and are, in fact, central to the entire argument of this book. The problem with which Americans are now wrestling is the problem of finding *enough* demand to buy all the things that we are capable of producing. This is the precise opposite of the kind of inflationary situation in which the problem is too much demand relative to production. In other words, the fact that we have unemployed workers and idle factories means that the increased demand generated by a government deficit is likely to lead to an increase in *production* rather than an increase in prices. As consumers or businessmen spend their increased incomes, prices may "firm up" temporarily, but competition among business enterprises will soon lead to a race for more sales, and this will again ease the price situation. This process has been repeated over and over in recent years. Even if price increases do occur in areas where supply is slow to expand, experience has shown that, under peacetime conditions, such shortages seldom last long: here is where a free enterprise competitive system operates at its very best.

This can be carried a step further. The purpose of lower taxes or higher levels of government spending is to eliminate unemployment and excess productive capacity, to draw idle resources into useful private or public employment. This should be absolutely clear: continuous deficits or deficits for their own sake have no meaning whatsoever. A government that runs at a deficit when the economy is producing at its maximum level of output is courting economic disaster. All our fears about the inflationary effects of deficit spending are fully justified under these conditions.

The error that many of us make is to confuse a situation in which Supply cannot be expanded and Demand is rising with the fundamentally different situation in which labor and resources languish because Demand is inadequate. Clearly the prescription for the first case is higher taxes or lower government spending: these will repress total demands. But the same prescription can hardly be appropriate for an illness whose cause and symptoms are so diametrically opposed.

This leads to an equally important discovery. If prices rise because the demand for goods and services exceeds our capacity to produce as much as people want to buy, then *any* increase in demand, from *any* source, can lead to inflation. If we were to hear today that businessmen were planning to spend an extra $10 billions on new plant and equipment, or that consumers were about to go on a $10 billion spending spree, most people would cheer the good news. Yet, if the productive capacities of the economy were fully employed, this increase in demand would have just as inflationary an impact as an increase of $10 billions in government spending or a reduction of $10 billions in tax revenues.

The question of whether or not to give government spending "priority" over private spending is essentially a question of social policy. It relates to one's basic philosophical viewpoint about the relative importance of the goods and services provided by government in comparison to the importance of the goods and services provided for consumers and businessmen. Economics, however, is neutral on this issue. An increase in Demand, in excess of the economy's ability to expand Supply, will cause prices to rise, whether the dollars are public or private. An increase in Demand that leads to an equivalent expansion in Supply will not have an inflationary effect, whether the dollars are public or private. The trend of prices will be determined by the relationship between total Demand and total Supply, not by the *source* of the additional demand.

This is clearly illustrated by what happened in 1956-57, when the economy had little excess capacity or idle labor to expand output. Prices rose 5 percent over the two-year period, even though the federal government had a surplus of $5.7 billions in 1956 and another surplus of $2.0 billions in 1957. The reason, of course, lay in the rapidly expanding demands and expenditures of the rest of the economy. In particular, business outlays on investment projects ran more than $24 billions in excess of business savings during 1956 and about $21 billions more than business savings in 1955 and 1957— almost twice as much as in 1954. Thus while government was actually dampening and repressing purchasing power through its surpluses, the business sector was vastly increasing purchasing power through its "deficits." The resulting increase in prices was therefore caused by a private deficit-spending inflation, not a public one.

But another lingering doubt remains: doesn't deficit financing lead to an increase in the money supply, and isn't that especially inflationary?

Here again the answer is "on-the-one-hand-on-the-other-hand." The supply of money does usually increase when the government runs a deficit. *But it also usually increases when the expenditures of the private sectors are rising.* The increase in the supply of money may result in inflation. It may also fail to result in inflation. And just to make the whole thing even more confusing, inflation can occur without any increase in the money supply at all.

We say that the supply of money increases when we have more dollars to spend—that is, when we have more coin and currency in our pockets or when we have larger balances in our checking accounts. Since we obtain our coin and currency by making withdrawals from checking accounts,* it is really the trend of checking account balances that ultimately determines the supply of money.

The balance in our checking accounts naturally rises when we make deposits in those accounts in excess of our withdrawals. But most of the deposits that we make represent payments from other people, so one man's deposit is usually another man's withdrawal. How, then, can the *total* amount of money in checking ac-

---

* Some people obtain their currency by making withdrawals from savings banks or from savings and loan associations. But these institutions have the currency on hand for depositors by making withdrawals from the commercial banks in which they carry their checking accounts. People who are paid by their employers in currency and coin should recognize that the employers also obtain currency by withdrawals from checking accounts.

counts increase? When is one man's deposit *not* a withdrawal from another man's account?

The answer is that total deposits rise when payments to depositors are made by commercial banks *themselves* rather than by other depositors. When commercial banks lend money or pay out money to buy securities that they have purchased, the new bank deposits received by the borrower or by the seller of the securities are not withdrawals from some other depositor's account. On the contrary, they are brand-new deposits in the system and therefore are in effect an increase in the means of payment available to us for buying goods and services.

If the government finances its deficit by selling securities directly to the public, the money that comes into the government is simply taken out of other people's checking accounts, and therefore has no effect on the total supply of money. But when commercial banks buy the government's obligations, then the money going into the government's bank account is brand-new money, never withdrawn from any other checking account. This is what is meant by "monetizing" the debt.

Therefore, this curiously magical bank-financed deficit can indeed be inflationary. The purchasing power available to the government was not withdrawn from the rest of the economy, so there is no question that government demands can be piled on top of the demands of businessmen and consumers. This is precisely what happened during World War II, when the only way that the demands of the private sectors could be held down in the face of the burgeoning money supply was through rationing and other forms of allocation. When controls came off after the war, the enormously increased supply of money poured into the market places of the nation and drove prices up sharply and suddenly.

But *the supply of money will increase no matter who borrows from the commercial banks.* New deposits are created when the banks buy government bonds, corporate bonds, mortgages, and state and municipal bonds. New deposits are also created when the banks lend money to businessmen for inventory accumulation or some other business purpose, and when they lend to consumers to buy automobiles, cover medical expenses, or finance a trip to Europe.

In short, *any* source of borrowing from commercial banks can lead to an increase in the supply of money. This can hardly be an argument against borrowing money: we have already seen that our economy would soon fall into a deep depression if we outlawed all increases in debt. Since, however, the lending capacity of the commercial banks can be controlled (through the operations of the Federal Reserve authorities), there may be times when it is appropriate to force individuals and corporations and the government to borrow from savings banks and insurance companies and other individuals and corporations rather than from the commercial banks. This is one extremely important way in which the potentially inflationary influence of a government deficit or of the "deficits" of consumers and businessmen can be kept under control.

The crucial consideration is whether the volume of production is keeping pace with the rate of spending on goods and services. For the rate of spending can rise even if the government budget is balanced or if the deficit is financed without help from the banking system. If the money that the government raises through taxes or through selling bonds to individuals, corporations, and savings institutions is money that would otherwise have lain idle and unspent, then clearly the government is adding to the overall level of demand in the economy by gathering in that money and spending it. This can be just as inflationary in its impact as an increase in the supply of money. In other words, what happens to the supply of money or even to the national debt is an inadequate guide to the outlook for inflation. Rather, the focus of attention should be on whether the total rate of spending is running ahead of or behind the rate of production of goods and services.

The association between government deficits and inflation is therefore, as history shows, more coincidental than automatic. We have had inflation with and without government deficits, and we have had deficits with and without inflation. We have had inflation with and without changes in the supply of money and changes in the supply of money with and without inflation. We have also had deficits with and without changes in the supply of money.

Inflation is ultimately a matter of Supply and Demand. A deficit that leads to an increased demand for goods and services when supply can be increased only with great difficulty will indeed be inflationary. But a deficit designed to overcome a shortage of demand rather than a shortage of supply will not be inflationary. It will contribute to the rise in output and employment that is the very objective we seek to achieve.

There remains one last objection to be dealt with. It is the fear that an inflation will take place because the public will lose confidence in the government's bonds and refuse to buy them, thereby forcing the government to the printing press if it is to avoid repudiating its debt.

This is a frightening argument—and a curious one. Essentially it says that the nation will at some time cease to be a nation, that it will no longer recognize the authority of its elected representatives, and that it will in effect suffer a revolution.

Now it is possible, of course, that we will some day experience such a mass withdrawal of faith in the government. That would be the last day of the presently constituted Government of the United States, and it would write the "value" of its bonds down to zero. Simultaneously the values of all other securities would also be reduced to zero and a new system of claims would no doubt have to be devised.

This is not a pleasant prospect. But the apocalyptic possibilities inherent in such mass withdrawals of confidence are best avoided by following a course of national action calculated to increase domestic tranquility and the public well-being. Governments have never lost power simply because they borrowed too much money from their own citizens in order to help create prosperity for those citizens. They have lost power, suffered defeat from their enemies, and been overthrown by revolutions because they failed to respond to the needs and aspirations of their constituents. The threat to our financial solvency is not in the size of our national debt but in the masses of angry and frustrated unemployed.

A policy of judicious government spending and taxing, and, when needed, bold and large deficit financing, is a policy designed to avoid such a national calamity. There is no reason why it should fail, unless by deliberate and malicious intent—or worse, through well-meaning stupidity—a large section of the public is persuaded that actions taken in the best interests of the nation are really the work of the devil.

❧ VIII

The Burden of the Debt

Even if the economy is not blown up by inflation, many people are afraid that it is going to be crushed by the burden of the debt. That is, they *were* afraid until they realized—on reading Chapter Six—that there *is* no burden of an internally-held debt, that our "burden-some" government bonds are also held by individuals and corporations alike as *assets*.

Were we, however, to view the debt as a burden, we would be forced to admit that this "burden" has steadily declined since the end of the war. At the end of 1946 our net national debt was $230 billions; by the end of 1962 this had risen to $257 billions. But over the same period of time, net *private* debt had risen from $154 billions to $672 billions. And not only was the national debt rising much more slowly than private debt, but it was actually declining in relation to the Gross National Product. In 1946 net national debt was 109 percent of GNP; in 1962 it was only 47 percent.

But perhaps what we mean, when we talk of the "burden" of the debt—or anyway, what we should mean—is the burden of government *spending*. We can measure this concept of burden by asking how much of our total output of goods and services is taken up by the government (and therefore is unavailable to the rest of us). The chart on page 81 shows the path of government purchases since 1947. This chart shows the trend of state and local purchases of goods and services as well as the operations of the federal government.

Three facts are clear from this chart. First, government buying as a whole has been moving rapidly upward since 1947—total outlays in 1962 were nearly four times as great as they had been fifteen years earlier. Second, state and local spending for goods and services has risen much faster than federal spending since the middle of the 1950s. And third, just about all of the expansion in federal purchases is due to national defense —nondefense federal spending has barely increased.

This picture is very different from the impression one gains from reading the daily press and listening to much congressional oratory. To the extent that government is a burden, an increasing share of it is to be found at the state and local level, with federal expenditures for goods and services rising relatively slowly over the last five or six years. And while billions for defense have clearly been appropriated and spent, one hardly has a sense of a runaway level of spending for peacetime activities of the federal government.

This picture becomes even clearer in the next chart,

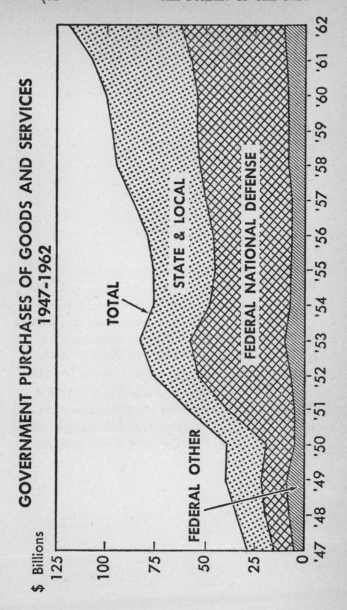

GOVERNMENT PURCHASES OF GOODS AND SERVICES
1947-1962

$ Billions

125

100

75

50

25

0

'47 '48 '49 '50 '51 '52 '53 '54 '55 '56 '57 '58 '59 '60 '61 '62

TOTAL

STATE & LOCAL

FEDERAL NATIONAL DEFENSE

FEDERAL OTHER

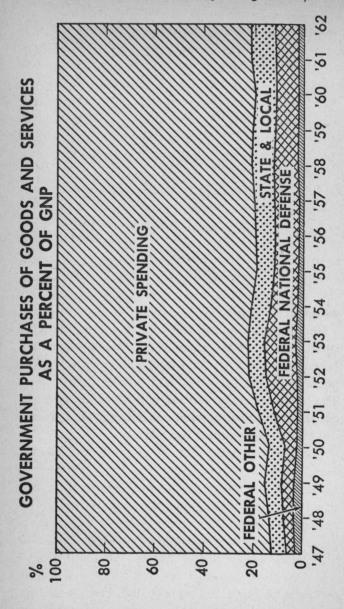

GOVERNMENT PURCHASES OF GOODS AND SERVICES AS A PERCENT OF GNP

PRIVATE SPENDING

FEDERAL OTHER

STATE & LOCAL

FEDERAL NATIONAL DEFENSE

which shows the same data as the previous one, expressed as percentages of the Gross National Product. Now instead of sharply rising lines, the chart indicates a generally sideways movement. In other words, the economy's total production of goods and services has risen just about as fast as the demands of our governmental authorities. In 1962, state, local, and federal governments combined bought just over 20 percent of the nation's total production—little more than the 16 percent they took in 1947 and almost exactly the same share as they have taken for the past six or seven years.

The role of the federal government's nondefense operations is also apparent in this chart. Only 2 percent of the Gross National Product is involved here. This is actually *less* than it was before the war. Its complete elimination, in other words, would release so little labor and resources for other types of production that we would hardly notice the difference.

But these figures still fail to give a completely accurate picture of the trend in government spending. Like all the rest of us, the government has to pay higher prices today for the goods and services that it buys. The increase in dollar outlays, in other words, tends to overstate the actual physical rise in the goods and services that the government has taken up.

The next chart therefore shows the federal government's purchases in real terms. This chart goes back to 1929, to provide greater perspective. Like the other two charts, this one shows the small size and minor role of nondefense expenditures—which are scarcely higher today than in 1929 or 1941 and which show little or no increase at all over the past fifteen years. Furthermore, while the chart on page 81 indicated that total federal purchases of goods and services have been on an up-

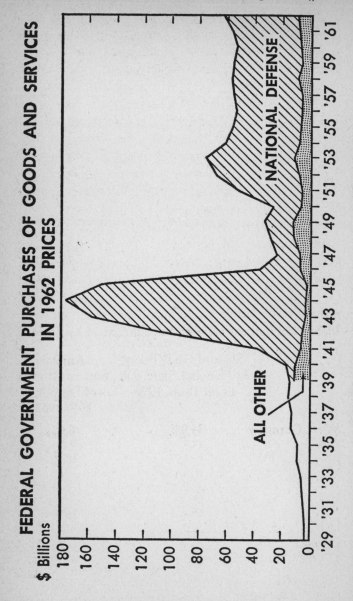

FEDERAL GOVERNMENT PURCHASES OF GOODS AND SERVICES
IN 1962 PRICES

$ Billions

180 — 160 — 140 — 120 — 100 — 80 — 60 — 40 — 20 — 0

'29 '31 '33 '35 '37 '39 '41 '43 '45 '47 '49 '51 '53 '55 '57 '59 '61

NATIONAL DEFENSE

ALL OTHER

trend since 1955, the chart on page 84 shows that this was due almost completely to rising prices: the physical quantity of goods and services purchased by the federal government in 1962 was only very slightly higher than in 1955.

In this connection, it is interesting to compare what has happened in the United States with the experience of other countries. Is our government taking a relatively large share of our total output? Is there any significant relationship between the magnitude of government operations and the rate of economic growth that a country can maintain?

A recent survey by The National Institute of Economic Research in London shows that eight major countries pay a larger share of their gross national product in taxes than we do in the United States. Since every one of these countries has shown a faster rate of growth than ours in recent years, it is clear that their higher tax burdens were no impediment to expansion:

	Share of GNP Taken by National, State, and Local Taxes, 1959	Annual Rate of Growth of Output, 1957-1961
West Germany	34.0%	6.4%
France	33.3	3.7
Austria	33.1	5.0
Norway*	31.8	3.2
Sweden	29.7	4.1
Italy	29.2	6.8
Netherlands	29.1	4.3
Britain	28.9	2.7
United States	26.7	2.4

* 1957-1960.

Since we are this far down on the list among countries whose growth rates we would do well to emulate, it is clear that the share of government in the United States cannot be excessively large. Indeed—could it be too small?

But the array of charts and statistics we have just examined shows only what the government has been doing in relation to the size of the economy. We have so far failed to come to grips with the real issue, which is whether the operations of government in the United States are a burden or a stimulus.

Either way, of course, the government acts as a great siphon, draining off money from the pockets of consumers and businesses, and converting it into spending for the goods and services that towns, cities, states and the federal government need and provide.* Needless to say, the kinds of services that these tiers of governments provide and the kinds of goods that they buy are open to political argument. On the one hand we have the philosophy of those who believe that it is wrong to use the income siphoned from the private economy to provide free milk for school children, while on the other we have the belief held by a few that it is wrong for the government to use the income siphoned away from the private economy for the purchase of

---

* Not all government spending results in the production of goods or services. Part is also used to make payments to people who give the government nothing in return. These are called "transfer payments," and involve no employment of labor and resources to produce goods and services for the use of government. They include such things as unemployment compensation, old-age pensions, veterans' benefits, interest on the debt, federal grants-in-aid to the states, and part of the agricultural program. In 1962, federal government transfer payments amounted to $43 billions.

missiles or bombers or other instruments of war. Both of these philosophies would like to see the government cut its expenditures—at least in certain areas. Still others would wish to have government operate as a more powerful siphon, taking a larger fraction of private incomes and spending it for public purposes such as conservation or housing or defense.

Here is the vital space in which reasonable men will reasonably disagree. Note however that this disagreement concerns the fraction of our total demand that will pass through the government—that is, the size of government spending relative to the total economy. This argument about the proper role and function for government has very little to do with the deficit or with unbalanced budgets or the national debt. It concerns the magnitude—*not the financing*—of the government as a mechanism for taking private demand and converting it into public demand.

The usefulness or un-usefulness of government spending in itself is thus more a matter of philosophy and politics than it is one of economics. Yet certain aspects of it should fall outside the area of dispute.

Somewhat less than half of total government purchases of goods and services (including state and local) goes for national defense. The British used to call such expenditures "dead weight," as they are truly a drain or a burden in the sense that we can do little to improve our welfare or living standards with missiles, submarines, howitzers, atomic bombs, barracks, and military bases in far-off lands. Yet even here, new areas of technological progress, new industries, new horizons for human endeavor are opening up. Furthermore, the knowledge that the United States is a powerful nation, well armed and well protected, gives a much greater sense of confidence and leads to a much greater willingness by businessmen to assume the risks of enterprise. Business would not likely be as venturesome if we were in a state of continuous anxiety about the imminence of invasion, subversion, or bombardment. No, even defense spending makes some positive contribution to the economy.

The remainder of government purchases goes in large part for goods and services that presumably benefit the community directly. Admittedly, part of this benefits special interest groups to a greater extent than some people consider just or desirable—we might instance agriculture, low-cost housing, or even the highway system. But one-third of nondefense purchases (again including state and local) goes for public education. Transportation—highway construction, maintenance of city streets, building of airports and water ports—takes about one-fifth. Most of the balance goes for such services as public health, sanitation, police, fire protection, prisons, public utilities, housing, community development, and conservation of natural resources.

To say that the "burden" of government is too heavy, then, is to imply that we have an excess of teachers, soldiers, policemen, highways, health services, weather forecasters, air traffic facilities, and judges.

But even here we have failed to come to grips with the real meaning of the word "burden" as it applies to government spending. Amazing as it seems, under certain conditions government spending might not be a burden to the economy *even if every dollar were frittered away on frivolous projects!*

When the government spends money to buy goods and services, those goods and services are obviously going to be taken up by the government and by no one else. If the labor and resources employed in producing those things might otherwise have been producing things for someone else—a consumer or a business firm or a foreign customer, for example—then we must ask whether what they produced for the government was more desirable than what they might have produced for their other customers. But what if there were no other customers? What if no one else would have spent the money that the government spent? Would the government expenditure then be a burden to the economy? In short, if the labor and resources would otherwise have been idle, was the government taking anything away from anyone else?

The answers to these questions should be clear. We can hardly say that government activities are a burden to the community when the community would in any case have failed to make use of the labor and resources mobilized by the government. Raking leaves, painting murals in post offices, close-order drill for army recruits, and subsidized public housing may strike some people as a poor way to use public funds. They may have a case. But that is something quite different from arguing that these activities are burdensome to the economy and that we would be better off without them: to prove that, we would have to show that the labor and resources employed in these activities would otherwise be producing things for customers other than the government.

In other words, when the economy is producing at high levels of output, when demand is running strong and straining our productive capabilities, then every additional dollars' worth of goods and services taken by the government does indeed take something away from a consumer or a businessman or a foreign customer. But if the economy is operating below its maximum and if idle workers and factories are available, then what the government takes, no matter how "wasteful" it may appear, is a net contribution to demand and will lead to a higher level of output and employment.

Hence the question of whether government spending is today a burden or a stimulus depends on whether or not the American economy is operating at something like full employment and capacity. The whole issue on which this book is built is that we are not so happily engaged—that unemployment is already a serious and prospectively a menacing problem. In the circumstances, we can be certain that government spending, even if it were for entirely wasteful objects, would nonetheless be useful *until we get near full employment.* Then will come the time to slash the wasteful projects and to make room for private activity. If we are not prepared, however, to spend enough money even for *useful* government projects, the chances are very great that we will never get to full employment at all.

❧ IX

Has It Worked in the Past?

Many people like to argue that what may be true in theory often fails to work out in practice. They point out that we have had deficits in twenty-eight of the past thirty-four years and that our economy still has problems. We tried to spend our way out of the depression of the 1930s, but we still had eight million people —nearly 15 percent of the labor force—unemployed in 1940. The record peacetime deficit of $9 billions in 1958 has been followed by an excessive burden of unemployment. Why, then, should a reasonable man believe that deficit financing, no matter how logically elegant the theoretical case for it, can really overcome our difficulties?

Perhaps a look back over the record can provide an answer to this question. Indeed, the historical patterns of the past provide abundant proof of the analysis that we have set forth in the preceding pages.

Take the case of the 1930s first. It is perfectly true, of course, that the United States still had a shocking amount of unemployment at the end of the decade. But the crucial question is the degree to which deficit financing was used to overcome the economic crisis.

The chart on page 93 shows the trend of Gross National Product from 1929 to 1940, compared with total federal government expenditures for goods and services. The lower panel shows the federal deficit as a percentage of the GNP. The story told by this chart is short and to the point: the operations of government were minuscule compared with the drastic collapse in business activity from 1929 to 1933. In fact, the business recovery seems to have taken place despite rather than because of anything the government contributed. The problem, however, was that the "recovery" never caught up with the rise in population and labor force, with the result that we continued to have desperate unemployment problems until the outbreak of the war.

Seen from this perspective, the excitement about deficit spending during the 1930s is difficult to comprehend. Yet one must recall the atmosphere of the time. Along with the complete shattering of prosperity both here and throughout the world, our financial system was on the verge of chaos and business enterprise was paralyzed. The sudden emergence of powerful labor unions (now no longer a novelty) and unorthodox political ideas were deeply disturbing to the business community. Deficit spending as a positive technique

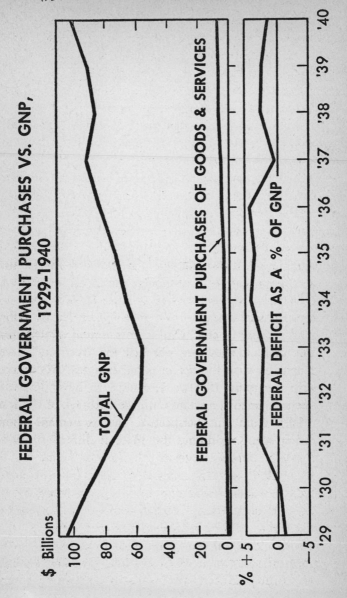

FEDERAL GOVERNMENT PURCHASES VS. GNP, 1929-1940

$ Billions

100 — 80 — 60 — 40 — 20 — 0

TOTAL GNP

FEDERAL GOVERNMENT PURCHASES OF GOODS & SERVICES

% +5 — 0 — −5

FEDERAL DEFICIT AS A % OF GNP

'29 '30 '31 '32 '33 '34 '35 '36 '37 '38 '39 '40

for curing depression was, in fact, an extremely daring and novel concept: Congress *raised* tax rates in 1932 and again in 1936 in an effort to put the budget in balance, most state and local governments were diligently running surpluses, while the first Roosevelt election campaign criticized the Hoover administration's profligacy and failure to carry out a "sound" fiscal policy.

The timid, faltering half-use of government spending in the 1930s therefore hardly seems relevant to the problems we face today. Most businessmen now understand—and the Full Employment Act of 1946 itself proclaims—that the government has a primary responsibility for the maintenance of economic stability and high employment. Federal government purchases of goods and services now run around 10 percent of Gross National Product, compared with only 3 or 4 percent during the 1930s. Both the nature of our current difficulties and the order of magnitude of government action are on entirely different levels.

In addition, our wartime experience shows what a powerful stimulus to the economy the government can be. Federal government purchases surged from less than $10 billions in 1941 to nearly $90 billions in 1944, from 4 percent to more than 20 percent of our total production of goods and services. The goods and services acquired by the government in 1944 exceeded the economy's *total* output of goods and services in 1934. The deficit rose abruptly and steeply, despite sharp increases in tax rates. For the single year 1944, it reached the astronomical sum of $54.6 billion: more than total government expenditures over the hundred and thirty years from the signing of the Constitution to the beginning of World War I.

But Gross National Product also swelled under the stimulus of government spending, as businessmen responded to the rapid expansion in demand. Civilian employment rose from 47 million to 54 million in four years, even while the armed forces absorbed an additional 11 million men and women. In 1944, fewer than one million people were unemployed and GNP had risen by nearly $100 billions since 1941.

Despite a rise of more than $200 billions in the net national debt during World War II, did the American people emerge poorer from this experience? Were we on the verge of bankruptcy? Was the dollar repudiated by all the other nations of the world? Of course not; we were about to move into one of the most prosperous periods of our history. Foreign countries were so desperate for dollars that we had to make large-scale loans and grants to them to enable them to cover their purchases of our production. Far from bankrupt, we were extraordinarily vigorous, powerful, and wealthy.

However, if the war had lasted much longer, we might have come out of it poorer rather than richer, just as many European countries did. This would not have been the consequence of the method that the government chose to finance the war. Rather, the problem would have arisen because the war effort itself absorbed such an enormous proportion of our productive capacity that we would have been unable to maintain our civilian factories and machinery or our stock of residential housing. The real cost of the war was not the debt, but the depletion and exhaustion of produc-

tive resources that could have satisfied the requirements
of our civilian economy.

The significance of this extremely important point
can perhaps be given fuller emphasis by considering
what would have happened if the 11 million people in
the armed services and all the factories engaged in war
production had instead been put to work to produce
roads and houses and automobiles and dresses and
shirts (and also the factories and machines needed to
make all these things). Can anyone deny that we would
then have been fabulously richer *even though government financing had been precisely the same as it was
from 1941 to 1945?*

The cost of the war, in short, had nothing to do
with money: it had to do with all the things we had to
give up in order to release the labor and resources that
our war effort required. The real reason that we were
so much richer than the other countries at the end of
the war had nothing whatsoever to do with whether
we financed our war effort with more or less taxation
than they. Rather, it was because the war took so much
less of a toll upon American physical capital.

Our more recent economic patterns are also instruc-
tive in showing the impact of government finances
upon the trend of business activity. A look at the following table shows that the rise in Gross National Product moves along at a more rapid pace during the years
when the government is running a deficit than when it
is running a surplus.

Here is how the data actually compare:

Rather than arguing against the success of deficit
financing as a means of stimulating economic activity,

	Rise in Output (per annum)
Budget Surplus Periods	
Dec. 1955-Dec. 1957*	4.0%
June 1959-Dec. 1960	2.0
Budget Deficit Periods	
Dec. 1957-June 1959	6.5
Dec. 1960-Dec. 1962	5.8

* From December 1954, a relatively low point in business activity, to December 1957, the rise in GNP was 4.5% per annum.

the record shows that the economy has grown most rapidly when the government was spending more than it was taking in. The reason, of course, is that the government was putting more money into the pockets of consumers and businessmen than it was taking out. The surplus periods seem to have a tendency to stifle or repress the vigor of the demand for goods and services in the private sectors of the economy.

Of course, this is no basis for arguing that we should never worry if the government runs in the red. This would be both fallacious and dangerous reasoning. The essential issue of government finance relates to the purchasing power that the government either contributes to or withdraws from consumers and businessmen. *A government deficit is desirable only when the spending of consumers and businessmen falls short of what the economy requires for full employment and maximum output.* When, on the other hand, demand tends to exceed supply, the government should mop up that excess by taking in more than it pays out.

During the 1930s, for example, the government should have added to the demand for goods and services by buying much more and by cutting taxes at the same time. During the war, on the other hand, the government should have taxed us much more heavily: because so much money was left in the pockets of consumers and businessmen, the government had to erect a complicated and cumbersome network of rationing and price controls to hold demand down to some semblance of equality with the available supply of civilian production. Over the past few years, a more vigorous rate of economic growth could have been achieved if the government had contributed more to and withdrawn less from the private sectors.

Thus deficit financing can markedly stimulate the economy when it is used under the proper conditions. An obsessive fascination with balanced budgets and repayment of the national debt, on the other hand, can have serious consequences for an economy in which consumer and investment demands are inadequate to provide full employment and maximum output.

X

Foreign
Complications

No survey of the question of government spending would be complete without some consideration of its international aspects. Unavoidably these are of a somewhat more complex nature than the problems heretofore discussed. Hence we have put them into this chapter, where readers may study them or not, as they wish.

The fears about the international repercussions of deficit spending are that we will be forced to devalue the dollar, that we will have to repudiate our obligations to the other countries, and finally, that gold will pour out of our country, leading to a complete breakdown of the currency.

These fears have little basis in fact. The balance

between what our government spends and what it receives in the form of tax revenues is only indirectly, and frequently only coincidentally, related to the international balance of payments—that is, to the difference between the amounts that Americans pay out to foreigners and the amounts that foreigners pay to us. Large areas of the balance of payments are determined by factors that have little or nothing to do with economic affairs at home, and, most specifically, have nothing to do with trends in government expenditures and receipts within the United States.

Recent experience is proof of this. The years 1959 and 1960 saw the widest gap open up between our receipts from foreigners and our payments to them: our international payments deficit in those two years totaled $7.6 billions. Yet the federal government ran a surplus of $3.8 billions in 1960 and a deficit of only $1.1 billion in 1959.

A look at several important aspects of our international financial relationships may add some perspective to these matters.

First, it is clear that our commercial trading position continues to be substantially favorable. Our annual exports of goods and services exceeded our imports of goods and services by an average of $4.2 billions in 1956-60 and by $4.8 billions in 1962. The Common Market area, for example, continues to purchase as large a proportion of its imports from the United States as it purchased in the early 1950s, despite the widely advertised fear that American goods and services would be priced out of world markets.

Second, more money would be coming in to us than we are paying out to foreigners if it were not for our military expenditures abroad and our foreign aid program. The deficit in our international payments is much more than accounted for by the annual outflow of $6 billions for these purposes. Of course, *any* item on the payments side is a drain on us and *any* item on the receipts side is a help to us, so that we are less than fair in singling out military expenditures and foreign aid as the major causes of our difficulties. Indeed, our foreign aid program enables many countries to make purchases here that would be impossible if the U.S. Government were not making the dollars available to them. But the important point is that our balance of payments on *private* transactions clearly shows a large excess of receipts from foreigners over our payments to them. Our balance of payments problem arises only because of political decisions, rather than because of domestic economic forces.

Third, we would still be in good shape in our international financial relationships, even with the military expenditures and foreign aid, were it not for the movement of short-term capital. This item represents the movement of money from one country to another seeking the highest possible rate of interest. American interest rates are low compared with interest rates in Western Europe and Japan. The authorities here have kept our interest rates low in the hope of stimulating domestic business activity. If the momentum of business activity were more strongly upward, interest rates on this side of the ocean could be allowed to rise, and then the outflow of short term capital would undoubtedly be reduced and the inflow of funds from abroad would be increased.

How does all of this relate to the question of a federal government deficit?

Concern over the relationship between government fiscal policy and the balance of international payments is concentrated in two main areas. First, it is feared that inflation will price American goods out of world markets and thus choke off our export trade while stimulating imports. Second, we hear that foreigners will be so frightened by a large federal deficit that they will cash in all their dollars and take their money out in the form of gold.

The first ground for concern—the fear of inflation and its impact on the balance of payments—we can quickly dismiss. As we have already seen, a widespread or substantial inflation is an unlikely consequence of a rise in deficit financing under current conditions of unemployment. Furthermore, if inflation is a threat, it would occur as a result of *any* increase in business activity, whether the impetus came from an increase in government demand or from private demand.

Rising levels of business activity do of course lead to increased imports into the United States. Each increase of $1 billion in Gross National Product tends to attract an additional $40 millions of imports from abroad. But this "propensity" to import more as our incomes rise is not likely to result in any serious deterioration in the balance of payments.

Indeed, a rising level of activity here will encourage foreigners to invest in American businesses and the American stock markets; simultaneously, Americans will be more interested in making investments at home rather than in investing abroad. This pattern has been repeated over and over again all over the world, as investment capital moves toward those areas where economic growth is most pronounced and most solidly based. Furthermore, as we have indicated, a more rapid rate of growth would permit higher short-term interest rates in the United States, which would in turn dampen or reverse the outflow of short-term funds from our shores.

Equally important, in a vigorously expanding domestic economy businessmen are willing to take the risks of launching new products and of introducing new cost-reducing techniques. This will tend to lead to an increase in American exports of goods and services to foreigners. The point is proven by the recent experience of the United States in contrast to that of the countries of the European Economic Community. Slow economic growth at home failed to cure the deficit in our balance of payments, while an enviable rate of economic growth in Western Europe was accompanied by a persistent and substantial inflow of funds from the rest of the world.

The second area for alarm is the question of our ability to retain our gold in the face of the presumed fears generated in Europeans by our federal deficits. This objection, too, has little substance. For example, an article in the *Journal of Commerce* of February 27, 1963, reported on the "alarmed" state of the European mind in the face of proposed American deficits:

> It is a remarkable fact that neither the foreign exchange markets, nor the stock exchange, nor press comments or financial gossip has indicated such alarm to date. Even the Swiss bankers, sometimes cited as the ultimate arbiters of financial rectitude, and with power to enforce their judgment by with-

drawing gold from the United States, have remained calm.

The attitude of these Swiss bankers is less surprising than it might appear at first glance: European financial leaders have long been urging the United States to undertake a program of federal economic stimulation through higher expenditures, lower taxes, or both. A statement issued on December 13, 1962, by the Organization for Economic Cooperation and Development—an organization of Atlantic Community finance ministers and central bankers—made the point without qualification:

> A greater stimulus from the federal budget would seem necessary to offset the weakness of private demand, a stimulus that could be provided by tax reductions, by higher federal expenditures, or by a combination of the two. . . . The quicker the economy regains the full employment level, the shorter will be the period during which government deficits are incurred. It is greatly to be hoped that the fiscal changes to be proposed to Congress in 1963 will be adequate in scope and timing to permit the early absorption of the present slack in the economy.
>
> Confidence in the dollar depends in good part on a strong domestic economy; it is unlikely to be fostered for any length of time by policies which keep the level of activity low.

In short, while the deficit in our international balance of payments is indeed serious and calls for some important adjustments on our part, the effort to overcome it through a policy of balanced budgets by the federal government and consequent slow economic growth is likely to prove fruitless. Our fundamental commercial trading position in world markets continues to be strong. A more rapid rate of economic growth at home would stimulate technological innovation and thereby open up new export markets for us; it would also permit a higher level of interest rates and the retention of larger amounts of short-term capital. Finally, it is clear that financial leaders in other centers of world trade understand our problems and desire strong government fiscal action. The dollar will find its true strength in world financial centers through the strength of our economy at home.

❧ XI

Is There an Alternative?

Up to this point, our primary concern has been to demonstrate that deficit spending can be both desirable and stimulating to an economy burdened with unused labor and resources.

But now the emphasis must be shifted and the questions posed in new terms. The issue is less whether the economy can stand such-and-such an amount of deficit spending, but what is likely to happen if we undertake *too little* governmental stimulation. Can we meet the economic challenges of the 1960s and 1970s if a fetish of balanced budgets and a fascination with inflation dominate the clear need to eliminate unemployment and poverty in the United States? If the choice turns out to be between larger government deficits and more unemployment, which path shall we select?

Let us begin with an all-important fact. The demand for goods and services in the United States must rise much faster than it has been rising, if we are to avoid an intolerable level of unemployment. The reason relates to the curious age structure of our population. Because of unusually low birth rates during the 1920s and 1930s, the number of people of working age increased very slowly during the 1940s and 1950s. But the latter two decades saw an extraordinary surge in the number of children being born, with the result that the labor force is going to grow very much more rapidly during the 1960s and 1970s.

The figures are dramatic. From 1950 to 1960 the number of people of working age—twenty to sixty-four —rose by 6.3 million. But during the decade of the 1960s this group will expand by 13.3 million. Furthermore, until the end of the 1970s the number of new entrants into the labor force will be greater and greater with each year that passes. Thus, we must find a way to adjust to this abrupt shift from a relative shortage of labor to what gives every appearance of becoming a burdensome surplus.

As this flood of young people hits the labor market in the years to come, and as automation continues its inroads, we are going to be hard put to find enough job opportunities. To create an unprecedented number of jobs will require an unprecedented increase in demand.* In percentage terms, the demand for goods and

---

* Of course, it also gives us an unprecedented opportunity to satisfy our many unfilled needs, to eliminate poverty in the United States and help to alleviate poverty in underdeveloped countries.

services will have to expand at an annual rate of 4.0 to 4.5 percent. That is nearly 20 percent faster than the highly favorable growth rate we achieved during the decade 1947-57 and 60 *percent faster than the annual growth rate of 1957-62.*

Everyone agrees that we were expanding too slowly between 1957 and 1962 and that unemployment was excessive during those years. What few realize, however, is that we could still "get by" with that slow pace because the number of people seeking work was still increasing at a relatively low rate. But as the war babies grow up and start looking for jobs, the need for a more rapid opening up of job opportunities will be far greater than it has been. If the demand for goods and services moves ahead at the slow pace of 1957-62 and if improvements in output per man-hour continue about as they have in recent years, we will have *at least* 10 million people unemployed in 1970, with the number rising every year. One out of every eight people will then be looking for a job and unable to find one.

This will be a paradox indeed, for the *need* for additional goods and services will certainly have expanded considerably over the decade. The young people seeking jobs will want to get married, have children, acquire homes and automobiles and appliances. But need is different from purchasing power. Purchasing power depends upon income, upon being able to sell something to someone else, upon effective demand.

Can private demand—consumer and business spending—support an annual growth rate of 4.5 percent or more a year, the rate necessary to avoid the risk of mass unemployment? Such a volume of spending implies the willingness, *and ability,* of consumers to go on a ten- to twenty-year spending spree equivalent to the great splurge that followed World War II, when the money saved up during the war was burning holes in our pockets. It also implies a major investment boom by businessmen, lasting two decades or more, and much greater in magnitude than anything we have seen in the recent past, including the substantial investment expenditures of the mid-1950s.

Of course this *can* happen. But nothing in the experience of the 1950s or the early 1960s suggest that it is likely to happen without some additional stimulus. Government is the source from which this stimulus can come. A higher level of government spending without a corresponding increase in taxes will add demand from the government without repressing the demands of consumers and businessmen. As a supplement, a reduction in the rate and a fairer distribution in the sharing of taxes can help to increase the demands and spending rates of consumers and businessmen. What is important is that the demand for goods and services, and consequently the volume of production and employment, be made bigger by deliberate government action.

❧ XII

The End of
the First Lesson

Which is to be master, the American people or the blind forces of the economy? In the end, this is the economic issue that the problem of government spending poses. If the great lever of government economic power is firmly grasped and boldly used, the possibility exists that we can guide our economy in the general direction that accords with our ideas of a good society. If the lever is not grasped, or is only timidly used, the probability exists that we will be guided, willy-nilly, in whatever directions our economic machine discovers for itself.

Every indication now portends that our economy, left to discover its own destination, will not achieve the minimum objectives of a good society. The prospect already visible is one of increasingly severe unemployment, of the disorganization of youth, of the continuing existence of anomalous but indissoluble pockets of poverty. No doubt the rate of economic improvement in the future as in the past will be subject to spontaneous changes in pace, to accelerations and retardations in tempo. But the achievement latent in the "natural" forces of our economy is not heartening. It holds forth little hope for rapid, widely based, and long-lasting growth.

By way of contrast there is little doubt as to what could be done with a sustained, intelligent, and determined use of government spending as a means of stimulating the private sectors. Then the wishful projections of high growth rates, of full employment, of rapidly diminishing poverty—so unlikely of realization under the impetus of the unaided economy—come to be within close grasp.

What is to prevent us from doing what can be done?

As this primer has sought to show, it is not the difficulty of the economic ideas of government spending that blocks their public acceptance. It is rather the miasma of fear, the mists of confusion, the nostalgia for the simpler—but alas, unrecapturable—past, that make it hard to proceed in a rational way. The arguments against deficit financing and government debt, however empty of content, are rich with homely appeal, heavy with portentous warnings, disconcerting with their personal analogies.

It is perhaps expecting too much for a single lesson in government finance to dispel such doubts. To become thoroughly familiar with the viewpoint of economic analysis, to master the process of thought by which the repercussions of expenditures can be traced throughout an economy, and by which the public and private sectors and activities may be compared—all this takes continued study. But it may be helpful nonetheless to conclude our first lesson with a few points easily borne in mind, that can serve to refute the more commonly heard fears associated with government spending.

1. *The fear of large numbers.*

Without question one of the reasons that government finance induces feelings of unease is that it deals in such enormous numbers. Louis Brandeis once declared that no man could understand a billion dollars. It is little wonder that the contemplation of the awesome numbers of government finance—expenditures of $120 billions, a $300 billion debt—tends to upset us. They are too large to comprehend and thus they become frightening.

What we must come to realize is that a billion dollars —no matter how immense—is the only unit of counting with which we can survey and measure our economic system, much as a light-year, which is a number even less easily imagined, is the only unit of counting by which we can survey and measure the universe. Our economic universe is now of enormous magnitude and it is rapidly becoming bigger. Already our annual output of goods and services exceeds a half-trillion dollars; within thirty years it should exceed a trillion. Our national wealth is very conservatively estimated at about $2 trillions, and it too is increasing at a rate which could double that figure in a generation.

Against these magnitudes, the figures of government

finance become smaller—and if still imagination-defy-ing, a good deal less frightening. Thus a proposed budget deficit of $10 billions, instead of scaring us out of our wits, can be seen as an addition to total demand *of less than 2 percent*. A figure that once looked so vast suddenly looks very small. Indeed, the cogent question it raises is whether a deficit that will add only 2 percent to total demand will succeed in moving the economy as much as we wish.

2. *The fear of debts.*

It is understandable that as individuals we fear debts. Yet even as individuals we distinguish between debts run up by bad planning, and debts purposely incurred in order *to acquire assets.*

Much government debt can also be viewed as the deliberate expenditure of borrowed funds in order to acquire or construct public assets. To be sure, our particular budget system does not separate government spending on current account from that on capital ac-count. Nonetheless, the government does create public assets and does create incomes; it may ease the fear of debt if we bear in mind that a rising national debt is indicative of growing public wealth. Next time we are told that you cannot go on piling up debt indefinitely but must pay it back, we might ask whether this applies to A.T.&T. as well as to the U.S.A.; or when we are told that debts are burdens, we might ask why we hold such burdensome things as A.T.&T. bonds—or why A.T.&T. holds government bonds.

Much more important, of course, is the distinction between a private debt that is owed to someone else and a public debt that a community owes to its own constituents. A national debt should not be thought of in terms of a family's debt, or even in terms of the debt of a vast business. Backed by the power to tax and to create currency, owed to the very same national citizenry from which it is borrowed, a national debt is simultaneously both a claim on and an asset of the issuing community. It is thus fundamentally different from a private debt which is a claim on, but *not* an asset of, its issues.

3. *The fear of deficits.*

A deficit, in ordinary language, testifies to an inefficient business. Businesses run deficits when they are operating at a loss, individuals run deficits when they have gone beyond their means.

But this is not what the word deficit means in connection with the government—*or any full sector of the economy.* A government surplus or deficit is a means of balancing the whole economy, not just an expression about balancing the government checkbook. Here, too, we must remember that the normal, and indeed the essential, operation of the business sector also results in a "deficit." Just as we have come to see that there is an integral relationship between debts and wealth-creation, so we must come to see that there is an integral relationship between deficits and income-creation.

Can such a simple catechism protect us against the voices which tell us that we obviously cannot go on spending billions, that the accumulation of debts is and always will be the source of economic downfall, that a nation spending more than its income is irrevocably headed for catastrophe?

We cannot say. In the end the question posed by

government spending and deficits cuts much deeper than our understanding of economic ideas. It tests to the very core the most vulnerable of all the processes of a democratic society—the process by which each individual sifts for himself the real from the unreal, the believable from the unbelievable, the truth, however demanding, from the untruth, however consoling. That millions of individuals can succeed in this process is the rock on which a democratic society ultimately grounds its hopes. To the success of that process this little primer of economic reason is dedicated in strong faith.

❧ APPENDIX

A Test of
Understanding

As all good primers should, this one now presents a small test in which the reader can measure his mastery of the subject. The quotation that follows is a paraphrase of an address by a well-known and respected man who disagrees with the position taken in this book. Each of his arguments has been marked with a number. The reader should first attempt to answer these arguments himself. He can then consult our own numbered replies. Nothing would make the writing of this book more worthwhile for its authors than to find that our readers have put the matter better than we did.

As a practical businessman I have sense enough to know that when you spend more than you take in, something is radically wrong. (1) It's even more wrong that we are spending our children's and our grandchildren's money. (2) The history of deficit spending is a history of failure—we have had twenty-eight deficits in the past thirty-four years, to no effect. (3) Most of us do not worry about the debt only because it is so big we can't comprehend it; if it were smaller we would be more concerned because then we would understand its dangers better. (4) A few economists, I know, would have us believe that the debt is unimportant because we "owe it to ourselves," whatever that means. (5) Well, I have an old-fashioned conviction that debts have to be paid back some day. (6) If the holders of these federal promises to pay should lose their confidence in the government, we would have the most terrible economic collapse ever seen. (7) I conclude then that the greatest moral danger facing our country at the moment is the danger of deficit spending. (8).

1. Not wrong: impossible for any length of time. One has to *borrow* the difference. The question really is, can one borrow safely? Is it "radically wrong" for the American Telephone and Telegraph Company to have spent $7 billions more than it has taken in since the end of the war?

2. Neither the government nor the Telephone Company is spending our grandchildren's money. Whether the money they spend is raised through borrowing, taxing, or higher rates for phone calls and postage stamps, the money comes out of our pockets today. If our grandchildren have to pay off these debts, they will of course pay it off to one another.

3. Some of these deficits have been too small to have much impact on the economy. Even the $10 billion deficit proposed by President Kennedy for the fiscal year 1964 is a smaller proportion of the Gross National Product than

some of the deficits we incurred during the 1930s. In addition, recent experience indicates that the economy grows faster when the government runs a deficit and slower when revenues exceed outlays.

4. Ridiculous. To the extent that we worry about it, we worry because it is too big. But what does "too big" mean? Relative to other debts in the economy and to the production of goods and services, our national debt today is considerably more modest than it was 15 years ago. Remember that 95 percent of both interest payments and repayments of principal go to American citizens; if the debt is "too big," then we must be "too rich" because we own "too many" government bonds.

5. To whom do we owe it, if not to ourselves? Only 5 percent of the debt is held outside the United States, and this is admittedly a problem, even if a small one.

6. Of course, each of us as individuals has to meet our obligations as they come due. So do corporations and states and cities and the federal government. But as long as we continue to meet those obligations regularly and as long as we have the resources to draw upon to make certain that we can meet them, what is to prevent us from paying off an old obligation by incurring a new one? Many users of consumer installment credit, most public utility companies, most states and municipalities, and the federal government all employ this technique.

7. This is true of the holders of *any* security—that is why the stock market "crashes" and that is why runs on banks develop. Panic is usually self-generating, so responsible citizens should hesitate about suggestions of this sort unless they are on certain ground. Many governments have had national debts much heavier than ours in relation to the size of their economies—Great Britain in the nineteenth century is a good example of this—without doubts as to the soundness of government obligations ever coming up. Panics of the type suggested here occur only when the

government is overthrown or when the economy itself is disintegrating due to war, revolution, or some other form of complete disorganization.

8.   There is one greater danger—ignorance masquerading as morality.

ℰ Acknowledgments

The authors wish to express their appreciation to Professors Francis Bator, Adolph Lowe, and Seymour Harris for critical readings of this manuscript, and belatedly to acknowledge their debt to their former teachers, including in particular Alvin H. Hansen. None of the above is to be held responsible for lessons badly learned.

About the Authors

ROBERT L. HEILBRONER is well known for his writings on economic subjects. *The Worldly Philosophers* (1953) has become a standard introduction to economic thought in the nation's schools and colleges and has been translated into many foreign languages. *The Future as History* (1959), *The Making of Economic Society* (1962), and *The Great Ascent* (1963) have also found wide audiences both among the general public and in educational circles. A graduate of Harvard and of the Graduate Faculty of the New School for Social Research, Dr. Heilbroner lives in New York City and Martha's Vineyard.

PETER L. BERNSTEIN is that rarest of combinations, a successful businessman, a trained economist, and an experienced teacher. Also a graduate of Harvard, where he was a classmate of his present co-author, Mr. Bernstein is Executive Vice-President of Bernstein-Macaulay, Inc., investment counsel and economic consultants. A former member of the Research Department of the Federal Reserve Bank of New York and of the Economics Department of Williams College, he now teaches at the New School with Dr. Heilbroner. He is the author of *The Price of Prosperity* (1962), as well as many articles in the *Harvard Business Review* and professional economic journals. Mr. Bernstein is also a resident of New York City.

THE TEXT of this book was set in ELECTRA, a Linotype face designed by W. A. Dwiggins. This face cannot be classified as modern or old-style. It is not based on any historical model, nor does it echo any particular period or style. It avoids the extreme contrast between thick and thin elements that mark most modern faces, and attempts to give a feeling of fluidity, power, and speed. Composed, printed, and bound by THE COLONIAL PRESS INC., Clinton, Massachusetts.

VINTAGE POLITICAL SCIENCE
AND SOCIAL CRITICISM

V-212	Rossiter, Clinton	CONSERVATISM IN AMERICA
V-220	Shonfield, Andrew	THE ATTACK ON WORLD POVERTY
V-179	Stebbins, Richard P.	U. S. IN WORLD AFFAIRS, 1959
V-204	Stebbins, Richard P.	U. S. IN WORLD AFFAIRS, 1960
V-222	Stebbins, Richard P.	U. S. IN WORLD AFFAIRS, 1961
V-53	Synge, J. M.	THE ARAN ISLANDS, *etc.*
V-231	Tannenbaum, Frank	SLAVE & CITIZEN: *The Negro in the Americas*
V-206	Wallerstein, Immanuel	AFRICA: THE POLITICS OF INDEPENDENCE
V-145	Warren, Robert Penn	SEGREGATION
V-729	Weidlé, W.	RUSSIA: ABSENT & PRESENT
V-208	Woodward, C. Vann	BURDEN OF SOUTHERN HISTORY

VINTAGE HISTORY AND CRITICISM
OF LITERATURE, MUSIC, AND ART

V-22	Barzun, Jacques	THE ENERGIES OF ART
V-93	Bennett, Joan	FOUR METAPHYSICAL POETS
V-57	Bodkin, Maud	ARCHETYPAL PATTERNS IN POETRY
V-51	Burke, Kenneth	THE PHILOSOPHY OF LITERARY FORM
V-75	Camus, Albert	THE MYTH OF SISYPHUS *and Other Essays*
V-171	Cruttwell, Patrick	THE SHAKESPEAREAN MOMENT
V-4	Einstein, Alfred	A SHORT HISTORY OF MUSIC
V-177	Fuller, Edmund	MAN IN MODERN FICTION
V-13	Gilbert, Stuart	JAMES JOYCE'S "ULYSSES"
V-56	Graves, Robert	THE WHITE GODDESS
V-175	Haggin, Bernard	MUSIC FOR THE MAN WHO ENJOYS "HAMLET"
V-114	Hauser, Arnold	THE SOCIAL HISTORY OF ART, Volume I
V-115	Hauser, Arnold	THE SOCIAL HISTORY OF ART, Volume II
V-116	Hauser, Arnold	THE SOCIAL HISTORY OF ART, Volume III
V-117	Hauser, Arnold	THE SOCIAL HISTORY OF ART Volume IV
V-20	Hyman, Stanley Edgar	THE ARMED VISION
V-38	Hyman, Stanley Edgar (ed.)	THE CRITICAL PERFORMANCE
V-41	James, Henry	THE FUTURE OF THE NOVEL
V-12	Jarrell, Randall	POETRY AND THE AGE
V-88	Kerman, Joseph	OPERA AS DRAMA
V-83	Kronenberger, Louis	KINGS AND DESPERATE MEN

VINTAGE HISTORY
AMERICAN